when i put out to sea

when i put out to sea

Autobiography of Albert L. Loving

Herald Publishing House
Independence, Missouri

COPYRIGHT © 1975
Albert L. Loving

All rights in this book are reserved. No part of the text may be reproduced in any form without written permission of the publishers, except brief quotations used in connection with reviews in magazines or newspapers.

Library of Congress Catalog Card No. 74-82510
ISBN 0-8309-0124-8

Printed in the United States of America

foreword

One thing a person learns about Albert Loving by visiting with him for an afternoon is that he is an avid storyteller. Whether it's a New Zealand folktale, a parable to illustrate a theological idea, or an experience from his colorful background, he always has a story to relate. It's no wonder, then, that his autobiography is full of intriguing experiences and reminiscences like those he listened to around the fire in his boyhood home in Australia. With Loving's varied and wide-reaching background plus his gift for vividly narrating these experiences, his account of life is hard to put down.

In conversational style he leads the reader through his family background, his boyhood in Australia homestead days, his adventures at sea, his memorable experience in the Andes Mountains, his missionary work in Australia, New Zealand, and the United States, his account of the depression, his years of working with the Omaha and Oklahoma Indians, and his pursuit of archaeological interests. Probably as interesting as this narrative are the asides with which he enriches the book in explaining detail on varied subjects like pit sawing, washing clothes at sea, and baptism.

To a generation that remembers pioneering by Davy Crockett or Daniel Boone television shows, his accounts of homesteading and lumbering in Australia should be especially interesting. For readers whose knowledge of whaling and windjammers has been picked up in *Moby Dick*, he adds detail and personal experience from whaling and sailing in the South Pacific and around the Horn. The Saints will be interested in this account of the hard times of the church during the depression years and his criticism of work with the Indians. For the anthropologist there is reconstruction of the peyote services on the Indian reservation at Macy, Nebraska, that the author reported to Frederick M. Smith. Accounts of archaeological work in the Valley of Morelos, Mexico, should be of interest to archaeology students. And for the many people who know Albert Loving personally or have heard stories about him, the story of his life will be particularly worthwhile.

But the autobiography is more than a narration of experiences. The reader gets a feel for personality as well. With the rough edges of his background showing through to the consternation of more conventional individuals, Albert Loving's personality includes an unpredictableness that makes some people uneasy. There is a hint of taking action at times just to get this rise from others, but interplaying with straightforwardness and unconventionality is a search for approval, an attempt to fit in to some degree.

This trait of not necessarily accepting the customary is seen in his search for truth that he says has been a major influence in his life. He has been happiest when he has been looking for truth, especially as he has tried to find an answer to the question with which he was confronted in the Andes ruins, "Who were the ancient people and where did they come from?"

Putting out to sea symbolizes this search for some direction and meaning in life.

His affirmation that man is not the pipe dream of some god is evident. His unhappiness that man is not what he could be is also apparent. His hope for the future is to bridge the gap between the reality and the ideal he sees for mankind. Hopefully some of the truth he sees may help move humanity toward the ideal.

H. Alan Smith

acknowledgments

The preparation of this book is due in large measure to the fact that I almost lost my eyesight in October 1962. It grieved me seriously to realize that there was so much to be done in teaching the Mexican people and so much to be learned by study and firsthand archaeological digging. I used to sit and worry because I was fearful that total blindness would overtake me within a few months. It was while I was wallowing in the doldrums of this affliction that an old friend and author of books, Ivan Drift, stimulated me to try to write. We discussed practically every phase of anthropology and religion in this volume. Ivan would say, "Albert, if you do not write your ideas on the things that we have discussed you will be shirking your responsibility to the present and future generations."

I express sincere appreciation and gratitude to Gladys Mae Walter, Diana Cozad, and H. Alan Smith for the many hours they spent correcting and retyping the manuscript.

And, after a long and varied life, I am keenly aware of the fact that in the give-and-take process I have gained much from others, unnamed here, who also have helped make this book possible.

introduction

In my early youth I read in a book entitled *Peter Boston* the following statement: "Incredulity is the foundation of knowledge." While working on a B.A. degree in general anthropology in the National University in Mexico some years ago, I took several semesters in the history of art under a *maestra* who used to say, in effect, "If any of you students cannot endure pain, you have no business in this class—for the pathway to knowledge is a painful one."

Since my youth I have been of a questioning nature. Now in my old age I am thankful that this disposition has characterized my life. Truth is very valuable to me. In fact, if I were to state simply what I feel has been my driving force it would be: Seek the Truth in all avenues of life. Pursue it with all the faculties of your being. When you find it, live by it.

I remember reading many years ago the statement, "When God created man, did he dip the pipe of his power into the cauldron of matter and blow soap bubbles?" It is my hope that this volume gives a decided "No!" as answer to that question.

1

The roots of my family tree, admittedly gnarled and twisted in spots but withal stubbornly persistent, "ran over the wall" from Finland to Sweden, from the British Isles to Australia, from America and to Mexico. Both strengths and weaknesses lay hidden under each limb's tough bark, but for the most part my ancestors were hardy pioneers; they had to be to survive.

A sturdy root in this tree was my maternal great-grandfather, James Walker, who brought his young wife, the former Jane Wiseman, to Australia from the Emerald Isle. They became the parents of a son, James, and three daughters: Mariah (later Mrs. William Brown); Jane (Mrs. Donald McKay); and Sarah Ann (Mrs. Martin Luther Ballard).

My mother was one of fourteen children born to Martin Luther and Sarah Ballard. Along little Dingo Creek, a stream flowing into the Manning River in New South Wales, Australia, my grandparents reared their brood of seven sons and seven daughters, farming in a primitive way the rich alluvial flats along the creek banks. The seven sons were Lewis, Edward, Amos, Markham, George and William (twins), and Robert. The daughters were Mary, Bella, Lydia (my mother), Ada, Edith, Emily, and Alice. Alice, the youngest, is still living at this writing.

My hard-working, simple-living grandparents and their neighbors literally lived off the land. They plowed with either a yoke of oxen or a team of draft horses. But "man does not live by bread alone." Into this simple life of the pioneers came Elder Glaud Rodger, a missionary of the Reorganized Church of Jesus Christ of Latter Day Saints, with headquarters in Lamoni, Iowa, teaching the restored gospel message. Grandpa and Grandma Ballard went to the schoolhouse to hear the preacher with the new message and many times invited him into their home. Grandpa was present at a debate between a Presbyterian minister and Elder Rodger, out of which the Scottish coal-mining missionary came pleasingly victorious. Elder Rodger confounded the opposing minister with his power of delivery and his knowledge of the Bible.

After a year of investigating and contact with the RLDS church, Martin and several members of his family were baptized. The ordinance was performed in the waters of Dingo Creek and the confirmation service was held at the water's edge, May 14, 1876. He was ordained an elder, April 15, 1877. Martin Luther Ballard performed his sacred duties as a member of the priesthood faithfully and remained true to his covenant with Christ the rest of his life. He preached with power and assurance about his faith in Christ, the fundamentals of the gospel (Hebrews 6:1 and 2), and the gift of the Holy Spirit.

The result of his earnest and consecrated conviction to Christ was made manifest in his own family. Four of his sons were ordained to the office of elder, and many of his grandsons and great-grandsons are serving the church today as ordained ministers. Many people were led to know God through his testimony and preaching.

About a year after Grandpa Martin Luther had united with the Reorganization, he rounded up his family and moved up the coast from the Manning River to the headwaters of the Nambucca (crooked) River. All three brothers-in-law and their families were in the caravan of covered wagons, some drawn by oxen, some by horses, bound for a spot called Argents Hill. Here "selections" (homesteads) were available.

It was an arduous journey of two hundred and fifty miles in rocking oxen or horse-drawn wagons, and the families of Donald McKay, William Brown, and Martin Luther Ballard were happy to arrive at their destination. Out of gratitude for divine guidance and because of the love for the gospel, they made the erection of a church one of their first building enterprises.

Native hardwood timber was abundant, and all the lumber for the church at Argent's Hill was pit sawed* by these "bushmen" (sons of the forest) as they called themselves.

Most of these hardy pioneers (and there was no

---

*A pit would be dug long enough for the log—five to eight feet in diameter—and deep enough to be comfortable for a man to stand under the log. Over the pit was built a rack of small logs stout enough to carry the weight of the log when it was rolled onto it. If many logs were to be sawed at the same location, the pit was dug on a gentle slope, for it was easier to roll the logs onto the rack. When the log was in place, it was chocked on both sides so it would not tilt. Finally the log was chalklined on both sides so that the man on top and the man underneath could see where to guide the saw.

place here for softies) were excellent pit-saw men. Their first marketable produce was cedar lumber made from giant trees which grew five to eight feet in diameter. The logs were too big to be loaded on a wagonbed; therefore, it was necessary to pit saw them into "balks" or "fletches."

These balks were rafted downstream and loaded on the little coastal steam freighters bound for Sydney. Five shillings a hundred was the top price lumber merchants in Sydney paid for this beautiful red lumber. Half a century later, the grandsons of those pioneers went back over the valleys, dug up the stumps and roots of those trees, and were paid five pounds a hundred feet for them. It is doubtful if one living specimen of those giant cedars can be found today on the Nambucca River. What had taken nature thousands of years to grow, men destroyed in one generation.

Martin Luther Ballard finished his life of service in these valleys, faithful to the covenant he had made with Christ in the waters of Dingo Creek. The influence of his preaching and the example of his living are still felt in that part of the world which his life

---

The pit saw itself was a heavy instrument about eight feet long with a ten-inch heel which tapered toward the tail to four inches. Operating the saw was a backbreaking task. The man on top had to stand squarely on the log with the saw handles firmly grasped in each hand. The man beneath had a smaller handle attached to a movable box clamped to the tail of the saw. The two men, one on top and the other below in the pit, formed a human saw frame; it was their job to see that the frame was sufficiently oiled and powered.

touched. My vivid boyish memories of his funeral have remained with me. The stream of people who had come to pay their respects was a mile and a half long.

The other half of my family tree originated in another part of the world. My paternal great-grandparents hailed from Helsinki, Finland. They settled in Gripsholm Mariefred, Sweden, where they established an iron foundry.

My father, Carl Alfred Lofving, son of Andrew Peter and Clara Lovisa Wingstedt Lofving, was born there on March 22, 1858. Apparently he had little knowledge of his forebears. I do not recall ever hearing him mention his grandfather's Christian name. He did remember one thing, however—going with his father to visit relatives in Stockholm. He was impressed by the apparent wealth of the people with whom they stayed. The house was an imposing affair set in spacious grounds and gardens. He was left in a small room while his father was elsewhere, and he remembered that with childlike curiosity he had examined everything in it; all the furnishings were elaborate. After a long time his father came back, took him by the hand, and they left. He remembered that as they passed through the gateway his father was weeping as he turned back and said, "My son, all that you see there by right should be ours, but I cannot prove my identity."

Years later, when he became a naturalized citizen of Australia, my father had his name changed from "Lofving" to "Loving." In keeping with the Swedish and Finnish pronunciation, however, the name should have been "Luving."

My father's adventures took him into many ports and avenues of experimentation. At that time many Swedish youth had to go to sea or starve, so Father became a seaman on the *Cutty Sark*, sailing between London and Shanghai. In 1872 the *Cutty Sark* and her sister ship, *Thermopylae*, engaged in one of the longest sailing races in history between the two ports. The *Thermopylae* won the race in a hundred and fifteen days. The *Cutty Sark* had lost six days while a jury rudder was being made to replace the original lost in a heavy sea. Mr. Goddard* of the National Maritime Museum says, "Without the accident, she would almost surely have won easily." These clippers sailed from the Far East around the Cape of Good Hope to England. They did not sail around Cape Horn into the Atlantic Ocean as some "wind jammers"** of modern day affirm.

When steamships and the Suez Canal later took over the China tea trade, these hardy seamen turned their attention to the Australian wheat and wool trade. The route meant rounding the Horn on the voyage out and again on the run home.

Father began to seek a wider horizon of economic opportunity when he became disgruntled with the wages paid by the British shipping company of two

---

*See appendix A for a letter from Mr. Goddard with an accurate description of the time the ships were built, a detailed plan of the dimensions of each ship, and the facts about the race.

**Fresh water sailors who talk out of all of their mouths at once without understanding.

pounds, ten shillings a month. A favorite trick of the shellbacks, as the seamen were called, was to abandon ship in Australian ports, hide out until the ship had sailed for home, then come out of hiding and sign on with another ship for more money. Sometimes they were paid one hundred pounds sterling for the run home.

Thus when the *Thermopylae*, the ship to which my father was then assigned, lay at anchor in Port Melbourne with hatches battened down and ready to sail, he made his escape. "Charley," as he was called, had made his plans when he had been ashore that afternoon and purchased a flask of brandy. Now, when the tide was in the ebb and he dared leave his post of duty, he went aft and presented the old bos'n with the flask. Having made his preparations in the forecastle by tying a few clothes and a pair of work boots into a bundle that he could throw over his shoulder with a looped cord, he waited patiently for the grog to do its work; then he noiselessly dropped a rope over, slid down the anchor chain into the sea, and let the ebbing tide carry him away from the constantly policed waterfront. As daylight began to break and the flow of the tide set in, he headed for a rocky point. A smooth beach lay just beyond, and he walked ashore.

He wrung the water out of his clothes, dressed, put on his boots, and began the long trek northward away from Port Melbourne. About midday he left the beach and headed into the bush. Toward nightfall the barking of dogs and the cackling of a disturbed fowl told him the general direction to take to a settler's cabin.

2

The settler's family was startled to see a young man, shabbily dressed, come striding out of the forest into the clearing. With broken English and much gesturing, Charley managed to make his need known. First came the food: a large platter of eggs, boiled salt pork, and homemade "damper"—a bread cooked in the ashes. Later he was given a reasonably comfortable bed on a lean-to veranda. He thanked his hosts upon retiring and explained, more by action than words, that he wanted to be on his way by daylight.

The next morning he slipped quietly away, heading into the fifty miles of trail that would take him to Warragul ("wild horse"). This rough wagon road was the main route to Warragul, up Gippsland way and directly opposite from the port of Melbourne.

Striding through the forest of giant gum trees, Charley marveled at their majestic height. He thought that they must be the tallest trees in the world, as indeed he was to later learn they were. Footsore and weary, the young Swede finally reached Warragul. There he was immediately employed as a pick and shovel hand worker on the construction of a new road. There, too, he became just plain "Charley" to his fellow workers and fell in readily with the customs of the Australian bushmen. He also learned to read and speak English. This was a new turn in the road for him and a far cry from his past experiences as an able seaman.

Road workers like Charley were called "navies" and

were set apart from the rest of the natives by their dress. They wore nothing but shirt, pants, and hobnailed boots. The pants were held in place by suspenders over the shoulders and a belt around the waist. The navies had strings tied around their legs just below the knees to keep their pants from getting into the way or dragging under the heels. These strings were called "bouyangs," and the navies were spotted on sight by them. This costume eventually became the natural style for the settlers, but the bouyang remained a mark of distinction for the navies.

It was on this job that Charley picked up a longer nickname. When he moved up the mountain to Buchan to do more road work, the title "Warragul Charley" went with him. During the next year (1886) he traveled, mostly on foot, up the Blue Mountain ranges to Tuncurry, a lumbering and fishing village at the mouth of the Woolamba River. On the alert for any hidden possibility of opportunity, he worked his passage on the lumber freighter from Sydney to Tuncurry. Here he found what he wanted, and, with the exception of a few short trips on coastal steamships, he never went back to sea again.

John Wright's lumber mill on the north shore of the harbor stood at the mouth of the Woolamba River which intersected Myall Lake and cut deep into the mountains and spurs of the Great Dividing Range. The hills and valleys adjoining these waters were studded with beautiful hardwood trees of many varieties. Here ironbark, the king of the hardwoods, grew in abundance. Alongside, and each majestic in its own right, towered eucalyptus, beechnut, yellow and white mahogany, grey gum, red gum, mesmate, box, turpentine, and red oak. On the alluvial bottomland grew cedar and ducken ducken.

John Wright, settled in the middle of this gold mine of timber, also owned a large flat-bottomed log punt with paddle wheels on the side which were powered by steam from wood-fed boiler furnaces. In addition, this shrewd businessman operated a small coastal steamship which plied between Tuncurry and Sydney, where most of the milled lumber was marketed.

Into this veritable paradise of promise walked Warragul Charley. He asked for a job and was immediately put to work as a deckhand on the log punt. Here he loaded and unloaded logs and handled firewood for the boiler. When the logs were piled high in the mill yard, he was assigned to the drying yard stacking lumber or making repairs on the running gear of the log punt.

Commercial fishermen supplied the local demands as well as shipping small quantities of fresh and saltwater fish to Sydney from the waters of the coast and from the lakes and rivers that teemed with fish. (Today a prosperous tuna industry is operated out of Tuncurry, and the descendants of John Wright build tuna fishing boats where, eighty years ago, lumber was milled and dried for a growing market along the coast.)

Warragul Charley found the social life of the busy little seaport town as limited as his leisure hours for socializing. People were constantly coming and going, and makeshift accommodations were the rule. Those who had a spare room opened both it and their hearts to the homeless who arrived at the door.

To relieve the monotony for the ladies, there were teas and church committee meetings. For the men who had time and strength after a day's toil there were stag smokes, card games, and an occasional Saturday night's visit across the bay to Foster, where liquor was sold.

Many of these pioneers thought nothing of walking thirty to forty miles. With automobiles, railroads, and airplanes still a part of the future, these indefatigable pioneers plodded on, building with the limited resources available.

Most of them had been born in England, Ireland, Scotland, or Wales. Some were just plain "John Bull" stock or the Australian-born progeny of the newcomers. The Australian Who's Who—had there been one—would have included such families as the John Wrights, the Ballards, the McKays, the Argents, the Churchills (distant relatives of Sir Winston), the Scriveners, the Browns, the Owens, the Sullivans, the Jones, the Walkers, the Wisemans, the Mills, the Pipers, ad infinitum. Occasionally there was a German family like the Shultzes or a Norwegian family like the Andersons.

Then there were the three Swedes: Warragul Charley, Laury Anderson, and Alex Seaburg. Linguistic relationships drew them together. They worked together, adventured together, got into trouble together. One Saturday night they took the rowboat that the mill kept for the use of the millworkers to the village of Foster, across the bay south of Tuncurry. The evening started out innocently enough. They tied the boat to a dock, followed the boardwalk to the post office, collected some mail, made a few purchases at the mercantile store, and paused in front of the saloon. Three pairs of eyes met questioningly—then with one accord the Swedish trio swung the doors and stamped in.

By midnight all the Swedish stories had been told, all the sailor songs in their repertoire had been sung, and arm in arm they seesawed their way back to the boat landing. They managed to get the knot untied and to get into the boat. Alex Seaburg took the oars, Laury Anderson sat at the tiller, and Warragul Charley stood up in the prow to guide the helmsman in the right direction.

The tide was low. A southwesterly breeze had sprung up, making the waters of the bay choppy. Most probably the boat went round in circles, for they hadn't made much progress when it hit a sandspit. Charley stepped out of the boat, gave it a shove, and pushed it beyond his reach. Away from the sandspit the other two rowed, leaving him behind.

It was dark and the wind was gradually increasing. Charley stood fast in the sand—shouting, waving his arms, and weaving on uncertain feet. The tide caught him and carried him out into the bay where he began to swim frantically with his clothes and heavy boots on. Predawn blackness settled over the bay, and swimming in the choppy water became more difficult. Worst of all he had no way of knowing in which direction he was swimming. His physical strength, already sapped by a day's toil and an evening of revelry, was ebbing. Death by drowning stared him in the face. As he acknowledged this possibility, all his past life seemed to flash before him.

He thought of his father and mother still living in Sweden, of his confirmation in the cathedral at

Upsala, and of the old priest who had confirmed him. All his sins, real and exaggerated, came up to haunt him. Then and there he made a simple covenant with the God of his parental teaching: "O Lord, my God, my life is as open to you as the water is to receive my body. I have not always done as well as I might have done. My sins are before me. If I am worthy of thy help now and I get out of this sea alive, I will try to do better."

It was a simple prayer of need, and it was answered. Immediately his feet touched bottom and he crawled out of the water onto the beach. With a last supreme effort, he pulled himself beyond the reach of the waves, then fell unconscious where he lay.

As the eastern sunrise lighted the waters some hours later, an old fisherman found him there. Thinking he had found a dead man brought in by the wind and the tide, he turned him over, peered down at him and gasped, "It's Charley!" He felt for the pulse. "He's still alive. I must get him into bed and warm him up."

The old man dragged the prostrate form to his hut, which was almost hidden in the beach tundra. He stripped the still form of its wet clothes and put it into the bunk. Lighting the fire, he quickly made strong tea and held it to Charley's lips, letting as much as possible trickle down his throat. Warmth soon brought consciousness back, and after he had told his story to his rescuer, Charley went into a sound and comfortable sleep.

The fisherman returned near noon to his hut to awaken Charley with more questions. "What became of the other two Swedes?" he wanted to know.

"I don't know," replied Charley, "but they had the boat."

The old man went on. "The police and several other boats are out in the bay with grappling hooks looking for a drowned man. When I offered to help in the search and asked them who they were looking for, they told me that Charley Lofving had drowned last night."

In satisfaction, the fisherman finished, "I told them that I had dragged you off the beach at sunrise and that you were safe in my bunk. When they heard this, the searching party went home."

Charley slept off his weakness and returned to his cabin before sundown that evening—a man spared by the grace of God with a promise in his heart.

John Wright, the lumberman for whom Charley Lofving worked, was an elder in the Reorganized Church of Jesus Christ of Latter Day Saints. The first missionaries Charles Wandell and Glaud Rodger had arrived in Sydney from Lamoni, Iowa, in the early part of 1874. Glaud Rodger, who converted my Grandfather Ballard to the Restoration movement, was a Scottish coal miner. He had accepted the message in his native Scotland in 1842 and served as an elder there until 1852 when he and his wife migrated to the States. There they discovered "Zion" under the leadership of Brigham Young. After a few years in Utah Rodger was convinced that he had gathered to the wrong Zion.

With some of his neighbors, he secretly left and moved into the San Bernardino Valley of California. There he remained, confused and frustrated, until the

Reorganization came with renewed hope and promise. After he investigated the authenticity of its claims, he was accepted on his original baptism and ordination to the priesthood, which had been conferred upon him many years before in Scotland.

Charles Wandell had been in Australia as a missionary for the Utah church. Upon returning to the United States, he discovered policies he could not condone. For a time he became a religious drifter, looking for truth but not knowing where to find it. Then he came in contact with the Reorganization under the leadership of Joseph Smith III, son of the martyred prophet. In California, he began to study and compare. Eventually he joined the little group that, motivated by a desire to find truth and freedom from false doctrines and aspiring leadership, engaged in intensive research into the documents of church history. There had been a great upheaval of thought following the death of the martyred prophet, with each sect that sprang to life claiming the right of leadership.

Wandell found two documents of special worth to him: a revelation to Jason W. Briggs received in October 1851 and "A Word of Consolation," a small tract drafted by a committee of three men in 1852 and approved by the General Conference of the Restoration in 1853.*

---

*Charles Wandell was not the only distressed believer of the Restoration who looked for a jewel in the sky on that dark and gloomy day when former members wavered between opinions. To such and to the present, "A Word of

A few weeks after Charley Lofving's deliverance from death by drowning, Captain Joseph Burton came to the lumber village and began a series of meetings in the little church made possible by John Wright's contributions of lumber and help, both material and spiritual. Elder Burton's meetings were a combination of preaching and prayer services. Not only did he preach the gospel but in the prayer meetings the gifts of the Spirit were manifest—prophecy, unknown tongues and interpretation of tongues, healing of the sick by the laying on of hands.

Charley began to attend these meetings, take notes on quoted scripture, and check them out in his worn Swedish Bible. Earnest in his desire to keep his promise to the God that had rescued him from a watery grave, he prayed and studied to find truth. One day he was stacking lumber at the mill when he paused and looked up to see the preacher striding down the road. The Spirit of God rested upon him, and he heard an inaudible voice: "The preacher is coming to see you. He will ask you a question. What will your answer be?"

The preacher turned into the lumberyard, came up to where Charley was waiting, shook hands, and said, "Charley, we are going to baptize some people this coming Sunday. Are you ready?"

Without hesitation, Charley replied, "Yes, Captain Burton, I am ready."

Consolation" is a masterpiece of hope. As church literature it should be studied by every ordained man of the Reorganization priesthood. It rests today in the archives at Independence, Missouri.

It was fitting that Charley Lofving met his future wife at a regional church conference. Lydia Ballard, daughter of Martin Luther and Sarah Ann Ballard, had been born at Bungay, New South Wales, Manning River, on October 10, 1870, and baptized at Argent's Hill by Elder Joseph F. Burton. Her father assisted in her confirmation.

After a year of courtship (mostly by correspondence) Charley and Lydia were married on June 25, 1889, in a double wedding ceremony. The other couple—Markham J. Ballard and Hepzibah Argent—later became known by young relatives as "Uncle Mack" and "Aunt Heppie." The officiating ministers were Apostle John W. Wight and Elder Cornelius A. Butterworth.*

---

*Apostle J. W. Wight was a son of Apostle Lyman Wight, one of the first members of the Council of Twelve in the Restoration. He was a close personal friend of Hyrum and Joseph Smith who died by mob gunfire at Carthage, Illinois, on June 27, 1844. I remember J. W. Wight very well—a tall, dark man, with a strong voice and measured hand gestures.

Cornelius Butterworth came from western Iowa as a missionary of the Reorganization. Both of these men married Australian-born women, and they and their families were intimate friends of my parents for years.

3

It was to the gospel taught by the Reorganized Church of Jesus Christ of Latter Day Saints that my parents were converted and to which they shaped their lives. My father's local library consisted of not more than a half dozen books; among them was his old Swedish Bible, a Martin Luther translation. I inherited it and have read and reread it. The many marked passages give mute evidence of his sincere religious interests. He was a keen student of the covenants of God to the house of Israel and the restoration of Israel prior to the second coming of Christ. He also had a well-used English Bible and the *Saint's Harp*, early hymnal of the Reorganization.

Another volume of great interest to me as a child was *A Pictorial History of the World*. This contained many illustrations. I was particularly drawn to the colored flags of all nations. Even as a child I sensed a kind of oneness of all mankind as I saw them there side by side. Pictures of European wars and of the house of Israel in this book also captured my interest. *Corbett's History of the Protestant Reformation*, which I still possess, was another book of importance to me. As children we were taught New Testament Christianity from these books and had it thoroughly exemplified in our home. We did not, however, hear much about the Book of Mormon, despite our close association with the Restoration movement.

After their marriage the Lofvings went to live on

30

what was known as the Dyers farm a few miles from the trading village of Bowraville, up the North Arm Creek. On this farm my brother, Cyrus, was born July 17, 1890. Fourteen months later, on September 30, 1891, I made my debut. Yet another boy, Earnest, was born before Florence broke the monotony of boy babies. She was followed by Adolphus and Amos; then another girl, Emily, was born.

These were years of extreme poverty for my parents. The rewards of hard work on this rented farm were sparse. There was no market for farm products except corn, and the distance this had to be shipped by coastal freighter ate up the profits. The only other modes of transportation were oxen or horse-drawn wagons and two-wheeled carts. The roads were mere trails winding along the slopes and through the tops of mountain ridges.

We managed to survive because Father was both industrious and versatile. To add to his meager income from corn sales, he contracted to build cottages, barns, and stockyards. Acquainted with lumber, which was plentiful, he became an expert with the broadax. Total lumber requirements for a farmhouse or cottage were cut from native timber. Ground plates, posts, slabs for walls, wall plates, rafters, perlins, and shingles were then tied with wattle bark* into bundles. This way they were easily hauled on a sled to the building site.

---

*The wattle bark for binding came from the acacia tree. In the spring months of September and October the golden flowers of this small tree filled the forest with a splendor of color and perfume.

Father met with some discouraging aspects of human nature in his building program. At one farm where he was building a house and was ready to begin shingling, he asked the farmer to get some nails for the job. The man brought a package of nails and said cautiously, "Alf, I have counted the nails in this package. If you lose so much as one nail, I'll deduct a penny a nail from your wages." Father assured him that he could not afford to lose a nail at that rate.

I was three years old when we moved from this rented farm to a selection Father had acquired from the New South Wales Lands Department. This homestead was about six miles from Bowraville up the Buccrabendinni Creek. The aboriginal Kuri tribe had named this creek correctly when they called it "pull out the fishing line." The creek teemed with freshwater fish—catfish, perch, mullet, herring, and eel. Here also the duck-billed platypus (*Ornitharus Arincus Paradoxis*) claimed a favorite habitat. A spiney fish which had stinging spikes was not native to the stream but came upstream from the ocean in times of flood. We called it the "bullrout."

When Father moved us on to the Buccrabendinni selection, we lived temporarily with old Matthew McGregor and his son, David John, who owned a homestead across the creek from ours. As soon as possible Father cleared out the scrub around us and built a new cabin of bark from the turpentine tree. Again we had our own home.

The cabin stood on a hill in the bend of a wagon trail. It was twelve feet by twenty feet with homemade beds and tables made from slabs hewn with a broadax.

The cooking was done under a galley outside where the open fire served a double purpose of cooking food and giving light for evening prayers and Bible reading.

To us life was never dull. Because of the fish in the creek and the wild game in the mountain valleys, this was a favorite hunting ground for the Kuri tribe of aborigines that lived around the trading post at Bowraville. In fascinated interest my brother, Cyrus, and I waited in a mixture of fear and admiration for the blacks to come to hunt and fish and hold their carrobarees.

The carrobaree ground was only a short distance from our cabin, and although we never ceased begging for permission to watch it secretly the privilege was never granted. The Kuris did not allow anyone to see their ceremonies, and Father respected their privacy.

The tribal chief was known to us as Dottai. He was old, curly-haired, and wore nothing but a dirty loincloth. While we were not allowed to intrude on his tribal privacy, he often did on ours. He would come and sit with his back to our cook fire and ask in sign language and grunts for food. Mother would fill a plate with the food she was preparing and give it to him with a big mug of heavily sweetened tea. It was a sight to remember. The old wizened chief would sit sharing our campfire and our vegetables and beef in his next-to-naked attire. When he had finished he would lick his plate clean, set it down with the empty mug, grunt his thanks, and walk slowly off to his gunyah for a nap.

Frequently, in reciprocal kindness, he would invite Cyrus and me to watch him prepare a large snake or

33

wallaby for eating. He used a quartz-stone knife to cut away the narrow strip of skin on each side of the snake; then he would place it on coals to roast. We had to admit it smelled good but we never could bring ourselves to sample this delicacy.

The wallaby was prepared much the same way. After skinning it with the knife, the old chief would hold up the intestines and smack over the luscious juices that drained into his mouth. He made a loud sucking sound over this ritual which seemed to enhance the nourishment. Nothing was wasted. The internal organs like the liver, heart, and lungs were put on the coals to fry a little before being eaten. The women (*djins*) were given the less succulent to cook for themselves. Tribal hunting boundaries were marked in the bark of trees that stood on prominent hills.

Father was constantly busy felling timber and clearing land for crops. One day he was working on the hillside about fifty yards away from the cabin when the ringing sound of his ax suddenly ceased. Mother, always on the alert, ran outside and called to me.

"Bert, run quickly and see what has happened to your father."

I started on the run to the spot where we knew he was working, but before I had crossed the clearing I saw him walking slowly toward me, his right arm held as in a sling with his left. Blood was running down his face. He got to the cabin without much help from me and dropped down on a bench where Mother hastily brought him a cup of water.

"What happened?" Mother asked, her horrified eyes

34

looking at the dangling right arm that had been shattered in three places.

"After that batch of flu, Lydia, I don't hear well anymore, you know that," he replied through gritted teeth. "A tall tree was hung up and I went to free it. I did not hear the limb coming." He stopped and made a grimace of pain. "Write a note to Billy Argents and send Bert to take it. Tell him to come at once with his horse and buggy. I...I have to go to the hospital at Kempsey."

Mother gave a cry of despair and put her hands up over her face. "Oh, Charley! Kempsey is on the McClay River." I knew and Mother knew that Kempsey was fifty miles away over wagon trails.

Billy Argents owned and operated an ox-team covered-wagon freighter. With the note tucked securely in my shirt pocket, I ran as fast as my five-year-old bare feet could take me to the Argents home a mile and a half away. The tall, dark, mustached teamster met me with the exclamation, "What is the matter, boy? You are white as a ghost!"

Gasping for breath I handed him the note which he read at a glance; he began to shout orders. "Larry, harness the horse," he yelled, spitting out a wad of chewing tobacco. "Put this boy in the buggy, and let's get over to the Loving place."

We didn't have to go all the way for, to save time, Father had followed me more slowly, holding up his right arm with his left. Presently the weather-beaten teamster had him in the buggy and headed down the trail for Bowraville. An hour later they stopped at Billy Sullivan's Hotel there and picked up a bottle of

35

brandy. Armed to deaden the pain, they hit off for the fifty-mile drive to Kempsey on the McClay River.

As a family we settled down to wait and pray. It was some time later that we learned that Billy Argents and Father had not arrived at Kempsey until eight o'clock the next morning. And it was longer before we could draw sighs of relief and gratitude when we learned that Father's shattered arm had been set and put in splints.

Although Mother and we children were resigned to waiting, there was one member of the family that was not. Before he married, Father had an old dog named Ponto, and although Ponto tolerated the growing family he seemed to resent Father's attention to us at times. When Father and Billy Argents set off for the hospital at Kempsey, Ponto followed.

4

After he reached the hospital, the old dog kept discreetly out of sight for a few days, but when Father was well enough to walk in the garden, Ponto made his presence known. In his weakened condition—he had not eaten regularly during these days of hiding out—Ponto rushed upon his beloved master, licking his boots and hands and giving short, joyous barks. Touched by such loyalty, Father took his old friend to the kitchen and talked the cook out of some food. When the dog had devoured his meal, Father took him to the gate and said sternly, "Now, Ponto, get on HOME!" Obediently the old dog dropped his tail, bowed his head, and slunk away.

A week later when Ponto returned home, he was nearly chewed to pieces from fighting the dingoes.[*] He hadn't followed the wagon trail but had cut through the mountains in a straight line for home. Unfortunately, few settlers lived along that straight line, and Ponto came crawling in half-starved, mauled, and thoroughly miserable. He accepted food from Mother, then slunk under a shed and refused to come out except to eat. In his dog way, I imagine, he thought Father had deserted him.

Father's release from the hospital at Kempsey finally came, and he walked the fifty miles home carrying his arm in a sling. For months he could use only his left

---

[*]Dingoes are the wild dogs of Australia.

arm and hand, grasping a very light hoe to plant corn. No timber falling, no building. Our larder grew skimpy. To add to the meat that we raised and the milk that we had from our cows, we had to scrounge for flour and sugar. We partially solved the problem by grinding corn and using cornmeal instead of wheat flour.

When his arm was sufficiently healed and strong enough for manual labor again, Father immediately began to hew material for a comfortable home for his family which, at that time, consisted of three boys. About the time the new house was ready to occupy, my oldest sister, Florence, was born.

What a furore her coming made in the family! Aided and abetted by Grandma Ballard's tall tales concerning the arrival of the new baby, we were popeyed with enchantment. According to Grandma's version there was a hollow burned out in the box tree by the road on the hill, and the curlews had brought the baby there because we had no sister. We had heard the curlews whistling the night before and had seen their tracks in the dust the next morning after the baby was born. Besides, it was Grandma's story and we wanted to believe it.

Gradually we came to surmise that the story was merely an invention of Grandma's fertile imagination to appease our small-boy questions. When we heard the birds whistling in the same old box tree and ran to find their tracks in the dust the next morning, we dashed breathlessly back to see if the curlews had brought another baby. Grandma arose superbly to the occasion. "No," she said, "the curlews will not be ready to deliver another baby for about two years."

For some time after little sister Florence's arrival, the story of the curlews was a prime conversational topic at school. Then one day the school's reputed roughneck squelched Grandma's tale once and for all. "Why doesn't the whistling curlew on the Loving farm bring baby kittens, baby calves, and baby pigs?" After that no one mentioned the whistling curlews dancing in the dust at night on the forest trails. I never quite forgave him for ruthlessly exploding Grandma's beautiful myth, however.

Eighteen miles away the Ellis brothers operated two lumber enterprises. Father made the trip to Nambucca Head to make a deal with them and in this way got back into the girder-cutting business. Two men were hired to work with him in filling orders from Sydney. A new day dawned for our family—a day in which men and ox teams and high hopes were all over the farm. Although we grew most of our foodstuff, Father's new job would bring in needed cash for clothes and essentials.

Timber cut from privately owned land was not subject to government royalty fees (from crown land it was subject to two pence per square foot). Since it was to our advantage to acquire as much timberland as we could handle Father annexed more acreage a mile up the creek. The requirements were that we build another house on the new homestead and live on it. Although Cyrus and I were only nine and ten years old, we did as much of the construction as we were physically able to.

Both the house and furnishings were made of

39

hand-hewn timber. After we moved in, the girder cutting and hauling began in earnest. Except for very slack times, which were not frequent, the orders rolled away out of the hills at the rate of two wagonloads a week.

The same transportation route had to be followed. Ox teams pulling heavily loaded wagons took girders to the wharf at Bowraville. There the flat-bottomed steam paddlewheeler picked them up and carried them to Nambucca Head twelve miles downstream where they were loaded into small coastal freighters that completed the trip to Sydney. Once the lumber arrived in Sydney it was used in such things as warehouses and bridges around the capital city.

A special order for Allen Taylor and Company went to India. This was different and difficult to cut by hand. Each piece had to measure twenty feet long, fourteen inches wide, and seven inches thick. The cutting required much trimming on two sides, and special care had to be taken to prevent splitting across the ends; this was accomplished by leaving a full round piece of log twenty inches long on each end.

By age ten I was working alongside the men with a broadax three days a week while Cyrus did the farming. The other three days a week we went to school. There were four grades, and the school, with an enrollment of thirty-five pupils, was kind of a family affair since we were directly or indirectly related to every other pupil in school.

During my school days (I quit when I was thirteen to work in the timber with mature men) I had two male instructors, neither of whom made a lasting

40

impression on me as teachers. They were Dick Williams and Harry Crossman (who lived up to his name); both had been cowpunchers, and as far as I was concerned they still were.

One incident I particularly remember occurred while I was in the third grade. Mr. Crossman took me to task about something and, to emphasize his point, began to batter me about the head with his fists. He had named me "Pugnacious Loving," and perhaps rightly so, for on this occasion I stood up and pointed to all the big boys who were on their feet to help me lick him. We could have given him a good thrashing too, but he backed away. All my life I have resented injustice, lying, and hypocrisy.

The pioneer settlers of that period did not know the rich resources of the land on which they lived. Its productiveness was obvious when Father returned home from the hospital at Kempsey with the root of a banana plant. In three years we had all the bananas we could eat. The opossums had their share too.

Fifty years later those hills and valleys where we had hunted wallaby, cut girders, and wasted millions of feet of good lumber were producing tons of bananas. Few if any of the citizens there today realize that Charley Loving was the first to introduce the banana plant to that part of the Nambucca. If this story had been told long ago, my father might have had the honor of doing for that part of Australia what Johnny Appleseed did for America.

During my growing years Father was very active in church work. He served as pastor of the branch at Argents Hill, and at one time, before a severe influenza attack partially destroyed his hearing, he taught choral singing and band music.

Going on Sundays to the little pit-sawn lumber church at Argent's Hill brought both a revival of friendships and spiritual knowledge. We walked two miles through the forest, made a land of enchantment to us by wild flowers, birds, and an occasional glimpse of a kangaroo or a paddy melon. It was a walk fraught with anticipation for at church we would see all the clan: Grandma and Grandpa Ballard; Uncle Donald McKay and his family. From time to time we would eat with them at the church—delicacies of beef, pork, or chicken roasted in camp ovens, homemade bread, cakes, and jam tarts. And the billy tea...what a joy to remember! Sometimes I was allowed to help.

This was the pattern of our life until Mother's serious illness, which prompted the Ballards to do a thing that they had never done before. They told Father what should be done and backed it up with action. Brothers and sisters met at our house on Sunday and decided that Mother should be taken to the hospital at Kempsey. Uncle Bob went off to his farm and reappeared with his covered wagon.

Mother's bed was placed in the wagon and a chair was set beside it for Aunt Mary Gore who would accompany Mother to the hospital. Emotion was running high and tears of farewell were washing away all reason and faith when Father stepped into the bedlam. He held up his hand for silence and when the calm finally came, he thanked them all for their concern for his family and asked them to support him in faith while he prayed.

Father's ministry was like that. Everyone with whom he came in contact admired and respected his daily walk with God. Now he prayed while complete calm fell upon the listening group. After the prayer Uncle Bob mounted the driver's seat. Aunt Mary took up her position on the chair beside Mother's bed. Father went around to the back of the wagon, took Mother's hand and kissed her good-bye. Then he spoke to her under the divine power of the Holy Spirit and assured her that the children would be all right in her absence, that Aunt Alice—my mother's youngest sister—would look after the family well. Then he told her an amazing truth that later was verified: she would return home in exactly the same condition that she was leaving it. Bystanders whispered fearfully as the wagon drove away.

One month passed before Mother returned home— in exactly the same kind of health in which she had gone. Uncle Bob and Aunt Mary brought her home and told us sadly that the doctors could do nothing for her. She remained in this condition for weeks, sometimes seeming to gain a little, but gradually slipping back.

The task of attending to Mother's needs and doing the housework fell to me. Father had no other choice but to keep me out of school while he worked to make the living. In addition to Mother's extremely poor health, there were four members of the family to be cared for. Father gave up his girder cutting, laid off the hired help, and busied himself clearing land closer to the house.

About ten o'clock one morning Mother called feebly

43

from her bed, "Bert, run and tell your father to come quickly. Tell him I'm . . . I'm dying."

I ran the hundred yards as fast as I could, and when Father saw me coming he hurried to meet me. He was very deaf by this time and had to lean down so I could shout into his ear, "Mother is dying!"

We both ran toward the house, but Father outsprinted me, dashing into the kitchen, through the living room, and into the bedroom. There was no sound of breathing—just a ghastly silence. Both Father and I knew she was dead.

For a long moment he stood with his head bowed as though carved of stone. Then he raised his right hand to heaven and said in a clear, strong voice, "Lydia, in the name of the Lord Jesus Christ, I say to you, arise!"

Almost immediately, while Father still stood unmoving and I waited in a mixture of awe and sorrow, she stirred and spoke to us. A few hours later she was up out of her sickbed and moving around the room. In the course of time a tumor that filled a gallon pail sluffed out of her body. I had seen the power of the gospel of Jesus Christ do what no doctor could do. I had seen my mother healed and nothing could destroy that testimony. (She lived to be eighty-three years old.)

This evidence of divinity within our own gates and the faithful example of my father's life did much to prepare me for my own baptism into the church when I was ten years old. All my life I had gone to Sunday school and church services, and serving as an attendant at these functions was not foreign to me. But

44

baptism, I was told, was for the remission of sin; so, in my childish way, I tried to analyze sin.

Perhaps, as many children are, I was pushed by ambitious parents into baptism before I was able to sort out my questions and answers concerning that for which I was being baptized. Anyway, in those tender years, I had an exaggerated opinion of the ability of my father. I believed implicitly that everything his hands touched was made whole as well as wholesome.

5

My first grave disappointment came when I was baptized by Grandfather Martin Luther Ballard and confirmed by Uncle George Ballard. In my youthful love and faith I felt that Father was the one who should confirm me. I regarded it as his duty and my privilege that I should receive the Holy Spirit through his ministry, but it had not been set up that way by my mother.

Two girl cousins, Bella and Isley Ballard, and my brother, Cyrus, went through the same ritual at the same time. If it affected them as it did me, I never knew. Children do not talk much about such things, possibly because they do not have the words to communicate their innermost feelings. For years I felt a keen disappointment about my induction into the church. That disappointment gradually grew into indifference, and there came a time when I began to question everything religious—a phase that perhaps every youth goes through at some time though seldom admits.

My father continued to be my mainstay—my one slim hold on the faith. Wherever he was there was good but lively action. He played a trombone in the Bowraville Brass Band and, in an emergency, served as conductor. Cyrus and I accompanied him on horseback every Saturday night for practice. He taught Cyrus to play a cornet, and I tried to play a tenor horn. My ear for music left much to be desired, however. I was pridefully aware that I was a member of the brass band, though, as a pain developed in my right leg muscle from marking time with my right foot. (The muscle in my right leg has always been a little larger than the left—a gentle reminder that I once played a tenor horn in the Bowraville Brass Band.) The discipline of concentration that I had to acquire to be a part of that august body has stood me in good stead all my life.

Besides being community band instructor, Father formed a small band in our home as soon as Dolph and Amos were old enough to have the wind to sound a high "C". Had we not been born "too soon" we could very well have been the "Tootin' Lovings" of TV.

Father's example was one of temperance in all things. He was especially charitable in his attitude toward others. He advised us, "Let people eat and drink what they like. If a man does not know what is good for him, he will not learn by any words of advice from me." He was temperate in his dress too. To save his best clothes which were hard to come by and must be cared for to endure, he wore his work clothes to church. When he came within sight of the building, he slipped away into the forest and changed into the blue suit he had carried over his arm. Like the other men in those days, he wore a beard; I never saw my father shave.

He wrote often to his parents in Sweden, and in his zeal that they might enjoy the faith that had proved to be so great a blessing to him he tried to explain the fundamentals of the gospel to them. Answers he received from letters to his parents were always read to us in Swedish. The salutation was "*Min elskida son och sons hustru*" (My dear son and son's wife).

When his mother, Clara Lovisa Wingstedt Lofving died, Father grieved deeply. It had been his hope that some day he would be able to return to Sweden and see the loved ones he had left behind. He wanted to explain to them the restored gospel of which he had written. The only result to come of his earnest correspondence on religious matters was the news that they had joined the Baptist Church.

Lacking much in the line of public schooling, we received our geography lessons from Father and his friends who gathered around our fireside. Tales of China sea trade, the Baltic Ocean, English Channel commerce, Australian wheat and wool shipping made glorious listening for our eager ears as we sat around the hearth. What boy could hear stories of pirates, sailing around Cape Horn in winter, or shipwrecks in the Caribbean without having his spine tingle and the spirit of adventure fill his being? We listened openmouthed and charmed.

After one such firelight session old Charley Hendrickson, our guest for the night, tried to persuade Father to help him build a small sloop and sail to Finland. Father only smiled at us and shook his head. "No, Charley, my responsibility is here." And he looked lovingly around the circle of faces. Father's loyalty to his family was a guiding star in my life. I knew how much he would have enjoyed making that trip to see his homeland, especially to see his younger brother, Gustaf Anders, who was eleven years younger.

Eventually Father sold the farm on the Buccrabendinni, and we moved to the South Burnett District in Queensland. The country was entirely different from the coastal area we were accustomed to. The terrain was flat, giving way in places to low rolling hills and red soil. Along the river, the soil was black gumbo. Heavy pine forest covered the red-soil slopes and low mountains. At that time Kingaroy was a railroad terminal running from Brisbane into the rich pine lumber area on the Burnett River. Lumber mills were numerous, and great tractors fed with wood fuel hauled pine logs from the hills and valleys.

Our new home was located on one hundred and sixty acres of level land at Inverlaw, about twelve miles from the railhead at Kingaroy. The land was covered with heavy scrub. There was no pine, and the only useful trees were what the natives called "teak." We boys were put to work clearing the scrub from the land which would later be used for farming.

As a youth I was never particularly interested in farming activities. The stories of adventure on the high seas had stirred my imagination, and I wanted to experience for myself the things I had heard others tell about. I began my break with the family by moving back to the coastal area on the Tweed River in New South Wales, where I worked for several months at the Condong Lumber Mill.

Tiring of that, I left and went back to Brisbane where I shipped out as an ordinary seaman on the A.U.S.N. steamship, *Woodonga*. After a few round trips to Townsville in North Queensland, however, I became dissatisfied with steamship work and headed

49

for Melbourne where I signed on as an able seaman on the fourmasted barque, *Lucipara*. We were loaded with wheat for Callao, Peru—Land of the Incas. The sailing date was December 10, 1910; my life's adventure had begun.

I believe that divine will can shape a human being through his experiences for the life he must live on earth. Aiding this belief was the Viking blood in my veins that knew no fear and kindled the spirit of needing to find out for myself. It was perfectly natural for me to go to sea! My ancestors had done it for centuries.

The tugboat that towed us out of Port Melbourne cast off at three o'clock in the afternoon. We had eight able seamen in each watch. The first and second mates selected their crews, and I fell into the port watch with a grand old Scotchman named Major. He asked if I could steer. When I replied in the negative, he challenged, "Well, you'd better learn." In two days I asked him to give me a test at the wheel when it came my turn to take the helm.

It was like a dream come true. I was steering a big ship. For a few moments the mate stood beside me giving instructions about the correct way to bring a heavy ship into the wind. The order was to "luff her up a point, off a little." He explained that an experienced seaman could tell by the feel of the deck under his feet when the ship was off course. I soon discovered this to be true.

Our course for a few days was south-southeast which took us south of New Zealand into the Antarctic fringe toward South America. We were soon in the trade winds, doing what is called "running the Eastern down." The ship's log was registering fifteen knots, and we had a strong beam wind right all the way across the Pacific. The wind and the deep, long roll of the ocean filled me with delight.

Fifty-two days later we sighted land on the Peruvian coast. The dim flicker from the lighthouse made us eager to reach port, but it was another two days before we picked up a Peruvian tugboat to dock us at Callao.

Once in port I wanted to explore, so on the second day I got leave at quitting time to go ashore. This became a daily occurrence. I walked around Callao shopping a little, looking a lot, marveling at the way of life of the natives, and being completely enthralled by it all.

In my wanderings around town I met Andy, a Swedish-American who had just been paid off from a baldheaded schooner from Seattle, Washington, which carried lumber to Peru. Besides our personal backgrounds of similar nationalities and language, we were interested in the same things. The lofty peaks of the Andes Mountains with the rising sun throwing shadows through the notches and crevices in patterns seemed to prove that an unseen hand was wielding a brush with mighty strokes.

"What lies beyond?" Andy and I kept asking each other.

And then by accident or providential design, I came in contact with my first real experience with archaeology. Andy and I were strolling in Callao on Saturday afternoon, intent on seeing anything we could see, listening for anything that we could hear, when a middle-aged gentleman spoke to us. Thus it was that two young sailors, strolling on the streets of Callao, Peru, met the distinguished student of archaeology, Dr. Hyrum Bingham. He had been making some explorations in the sandhills of the coastal area near Callao. After a few minutes of visiting and an exchange of identifications, he discovered our interest in his findings and asked us to his hotel suite to view his treasures.

The amazing collection of evidence of an ancient civilization on the coastal regions of Peru held us in awe. Personally I was smitten with my own ignorance of the history of this people. I was a member of the restored church, that claimed to have the story of the history of this people in the Book of Mormon. Yet I knew absolutely nothing of it.

It took a stranger in a strange city on a strange continent to awaken my curiosity in the Book of Mormon to the point of research.

Dr. Hyrum Bingham showed us a hand—dry skin and bones—of a lady who had lived thousands of years ago. He had a sample of her hair—golden and silky. He showed us trepanned skulls which had been cut with a saw (and in some instances partly grown over). When I asked, "Who are these people?" my new acquaintance replied, "That is what we are trying to find out."

My searching mind had been aroused to the point of further investigation. After we left Dr. Bingham's apartment in the hotel Andy and I continued the discussion.

"They were just some Asiatic people who got lost at

sea and were driven ashore by the winds," he reasoned. But this did not satisfy me.

It was Andy, however, who suggested that I sign off the *Lucipara* and join him in a hike across the Andes. His interest in such a venture appealed to me, so we began our trip together with one hundred Peruvian soles in my pocket and an unidentified amount of money in Andy's. With high hopes and eager spirits we walked out of Callao. Many and varied were to be our means of transportation before we reached our destination. Equally varied were the experiences we shared en route. We rode in mule-drawn carts with friendly natives; we jumped freight trains. We ate and slept where darkness found us. Often the police picked us up and put us in jail for the night; we didn't mind because it was safer there, and we had shelter. Some nights we found a cave, built a fire, and slept by it.

We purposely let ourselves grow into the unkempt look that seemed natural to the area to prevent attack from bandits. In spite of our frugality, however, our limited funds ran out. After that we lived for weeks on dry bread, goat's milk, and cheese which we got from the Indians. We became very hungry, sold all our salable clothing, and asked each other if our quest was worth it. We agreed that we were seeing fascinating things, learning to ask questions, and even finding some of the answers; we were glad we had crossed the Andes.

At last we were between the Eastern Cordelleras and the main mountains in the Vilcanote Valley—"the holy land of Peru." Our hiking had taken us up the Pacific side of the Andes where more ancient enchantment awaited us. We walked in concrete aquaducts older than man can imagine. We saw immense terraces, and vegetable gardens still grew in those to which water was conveyed. We saw tumble-down fortresses built at strategic points. We saw stone walls stretching for miles over the rugged terrain toward the high levels of the Andes. We walked—literally—through a land of three-dimensional history.

6

The ancient cemeteries where tombs were built on the surface of the ground intrigued us, and we spent much time in these while vultures circled over our heads. I'm afraid in our youthful ignorance we plundered, pulling down some of the stones hoping to find trepanned skulls such as Dr. Bingham had shown us. There were plenty of bones but no skulls. Ascending the mountain after some of these fruitless searchings, we often had heated discussions.

"Do you still think," I repeatedly asked Andy, "that some lost Asiatic boatload of people left *all* this?"

He would reply wearily and warily, his eyes on the circling vultures above us, "Those critters are waiting to pick the bones of two misguided sailors."

"They won't get much off mine," would be my reply.

Two questions confronted us everywhere we turned, in everything we saw. Who were these ancient people? And where did they come from? One book that held a possible answer, and one to which I could have had complete access from childhood, had not been included in my childhood training. The feeling haunted me, overbalancing my rebellion for the church of my fathers, and I decided to give it a chance to prove itself once I again had access to it—the Book of Mormon.

Andy and I sat one afternoon on a rocky mountainside, too weak to hurry, too despondent to

55

worry, watching idly as an Indian funeral procession moved on the opposite side of the deep barranca that carried torrents of muddy water roaring down the canyon. The twenty or thirty people moved slowly up the valley with the corpse on a crude stretcher carried by two of the walking men. Every few yards the stretcher was lowered to the ground while the followers gathered around. Each took a drink from a large urn; their loud laughter and conversation drifted clearly to us.

Andy, his mind on his empty stomach, remarked, "They have drink. I wonder if they have anything to eat."

"Maybe we'll never know," I replied, my eyes upon the ritual taking place before us. "How are we going to cross that muddy stream to find if they leave food on the grave of the dead?"

Long ago I had quit arguing with Andy about the mystery we found around us. My questioning now was in the depth of my soul—a half prayer, a half baffled but genuine concern for the truth. Now, in retrospect, I believe that the actual turning point in my life's direction came that day while I sat in my weakened physical state on a mountainside in Peru watching a funeral procession.

From out of the heavens a divine power seemed to hover over me, then penetrate my being, leaving its imprint on my mind: "Could these mountains but speak they would give you the correct answers to your questions."

Gradually this divine influence withdrew and I sat as in a trance. Then, as men of old, I began to try to reason with myself. The mountains are older than any living thing: they must know who lived on them. But how can mountains speak? And if they did would I be able to understand their language?

Still shaken and thoughtful from the experience I moved silently to Andy's suggestions. We slept in a cave that night and the next morning mutually agreed to retreat to the coast. We both knew we could not endure many more days of hunger, and the vultures seemed to be circling closer all the time.

Neither of us was physically able to make the backward trek over the Andes, so we begged food at the first village we came to. With our strength partly replenished, we reached the railroad tracks, intending to jump the first train that moved slowly enough for us to board. This happened to be a passenger train, and we got aboard, pausing on the platform outside the cabin door.

Here the conductor found us when the train began to move and prepared to put us off. He relented when we made known by gestures our desperate need of food and help. He kindly allowed us to ride over the high peak and down the Pacific side to a switch engine junction named Casa Polka.

It was now dusk. I used one of my last resources for obtaining cash: I sold my razor. With the pitifully small proceeds I bought enough food to appease the pangs of hunger. That night we slept on top of the roundhouse switch turntable where it was comparatively warm. The next morning we got out on the tracks again.

A section foreman came whirring down the

mountain on his rail-inspection tricycle. When he saw us he jammed on the brakes and picked us up, freewheeling us down to the capital, Lima. As we rested and filled our lungs with sea-level air, our hunger lessened. We rode in burro carts out of Lima and ultimately back to Callao. Once there I lost track of Andy. I have never seen or heard of him since—another case of "ships passing in the night."

I went to a well-known boarding house for sailors and explained my plight to the manager, a hulky German named Kestler. He said that if I would take the first berth out of port that was offered, he would provide room and board and would collect my bill from the ship's representatives. Used to dealing with sailors broke and out of work, Mr. Kestler was not only helpful but a shrewd businessman. I had lodging and three meals a day, and I was content for the time. Soon, however, I walked the dock daily watching for an incoming ship. When none came I grew more and more restless until one afternoon Kestler said to me, "A steamship just docked and two of their firemen are in jail for mutiny. They refused to work in the stokehold." He looked at me and said, "You could take a peerhead jump on her. She will take you south to Valparaiso and back to San Francisco."

"I'd jump on an Indian canoe to get out of here," I retorted. "When and where do I sign?"

He shook his head. I should have been warned, but I wasn't. "You don't sign on," Kestler informed me. "You take a peerhead jump."

So a peerhead jump it was. I went on board and down to the stokehold, was given a shovel and told to

58

heave coal. In addition I carried ashes up the tween decks and dumped them overboard. I worked all night between the stokehold furnaces and the coal bunkers. I ate breakfast at six in the morning and went to bed in a bunk without bedding. At eleven-thirty I was rousted out again and sent back to the stokehold. Six hours on and six hours off was the schedule. I was still feeling the effects of starvation and malaria acquired in the mountains. Soon I was too ill to wash the coal dust off my face, too weak to get up and put on my boots. I was in my bunk when one of the deck hands came to tell me that the chief engineer wanted to see me.

"Tell the chief I am unable to get to the bridge alone," I replied. "If he wants to see me, he'll have to come here."

Minutes later I was dragged to the bridge by two seamen to confront the chief. Around the big black cigar in his mouth he began to insult me about my dirty appearance and demanded to know what was wrong with me that I couldn't obey his orders.

"Maybe," I replied, "if you get the ship's doctor, he can tell you."

He spat in my face. "So that's your excuse. Very well, You either go down to that stokehold and trim coal or I'll put you in irons."

"Throw me overboard," I yelled back at him, thoroughly aroused. "I'd be better off with the sharks. Do with me what you will, but I am not able to go back to that stokehold."

"So you refuse duty, eh?" he yelled back at me. "All right, Mr. Major, get the shackles."

In irons I was thrown into the wheelhouse where I

remained for forty-eight hours. Nothing was given me to eat except two hard biscuits and a pint of water. I appreciated the water as I was feverish and delirious most of the time. I remember little of those hours.

In Valparaiso I was released and ordered to take the ship's ferryboat ashore immediately. When I asked about discharge papers and wages, the chief engineer laughed at me. "You signed no papers to work for us," he snorted. "We never agreed to pay you wages. Get ashore."

I was learning little by little that all was not justice in the life of a seaman.

On shore I found my way to the British Consulate Office. The consulate general was absent, so the vice consulate heard my story. I sat down to wait for the captain of the *Bell of Spain*, the ship on which I had made my ignoble entrance into Valparaiso. I knew he had to come to the consulate office to clear papers before his ship could legally leave port.

When he appeared I accosted him with the injustice of his ship's dealings with me, but the insolent young vice consulate declined to support me in my rightful complaint, and the captain, triumphant, departed with his papers.

I was left sick and without money. This knowledge made me temporarily bitter, for I knew there was no seaman's union to reach into South American ports or to control English shipping. The *Bell of Spain* was an English ship under charter by Grace Brothers of San Francisco in a foreign port. It was also quite evident that the British vice consulate was bent on pleasing those in the shipping business. I had struck a snag.

60

I repeated my need for help and asked that he give me an admission warrant to the General Hospital in Valparaiso. At first he arrogantly refused, but when I insisted that as a British subject I had no other recourse than his office, he relented and gave me the necessary papers to admit me to the hospital.

"Thank you, Sir," I said as he handed them to me, "and now I need taxi fare to get to the hospital." This, too, he handed over to me, and by nightfall I was in the hospital. I never saw a doctor, but the nurses took my temperature and immediately set to work to reduce my malarial fever with quinine.

Three weeks passed before I felt strong enough to leave the hospital. I asked for a release, thanked the nurses for their kindness to me, and returned to the waterfront to look for another ship. I had no money; consequently, I went to Thompson's Sailors' Boarding House.

Thompson was an exceptionally large Negro from the United States. He was considerate and kind to me. I wasted no time in searching for work, and one day on the waterfront I met and talked to a Liverpool Irishman named Bill Brockley. As a result of this meeting, I went with Bill a couple of days later to the captain of a Spanish whaler who, we were told, was seeking a crew. Thereby began a new adventure for me.

The whaler was named the *Nautilus*, and the name was about the only thing she possessed that was fancy. She was actually a battered old wreck with rotten bilge timbers held together with copper plating on the outer skin. She carried eight whaleboats—four in the davits and two each in storage turned upside down over the cabin and the galley house.

If the whaler itself seemed motley, it was as nothing compared to the crew. This three-masted barque carried a complement of twenty-eight men and six officers. Captain Vollaric, an Austro-Italian, sported a pointed beard. The carpenter was regarded as a petty officer. In addition there were four harpooners also regarded as petty officers. There were so many officers and petty officers aboard there wasn't room for seamen.

The afternoon old Bill and I went aboard we discovered three crewmen from the United States; Jack Wilson, a boozehound from the U.S. Army; Charles Moffat, a Chicago bartender with a broken finger on his right hand; and Jim Ennis, a North Dakota farm boy of seventeen who was more acquainted with milking cows than working on a ship.

The Latin American part of the crew consisted of shanghaied streetcar operators from Buenos Aires and some outcasts from the Chilean Navy. To make the strange assemblage complete, the Captain took along his wife, a very beautiful Italian woman from Trieste, and his young son. The woman dressed well and strolled the decks each day with her goatee-bearded husband. Another member of the crew worthy of mention was Paul Byers, a deserter from Kaiser Wilhelm's Navy in Germany.

Visitors were saying good-bye to whaling friends and toasting hopes for a season's catch when Bill and I walked into the scene. Drunken men lay sprawled in almost the entire main deck. There was evidence of ferocious fighting everywhere. Blood lay in pools wherever a victim of a knife or a belaying pin had fallen. Broken bottles littered the deck.

Picking our way through the debris, Bill and I went below to check on a bunk in the fo'c'sle. We were looking for one near the good ventilation of the passageway, but this hope was soon discouraged. We were told to take what the Latinos did not want, and we chose to do this rather than fight for a fair deal. To bed down in the fo'c'sle was emphatically too much for our stomachs, so we went on deck and slept on top of the rendering pot roof. Here at least we had fresh air.

In the morning we were put to work to get ready to sail. We heaved anchor on an old-style hand winch with four men on each handle working the levers up and down. The anchor slowly left the mud bottom, and as the ship swung free in the ebb tide, I was called to the steering wheel and given a course to take us off shore in a direct line. The jib and spanker were set; the *Nautilus* was under way.

7

Then the work really began. Men went aloft to unfurl the sail. Landlubbers cleaned the messy decks from the previous night's brawl while other crewmen manned the pumps. The ship seemed to be waterlogged from the beginning, and we soon found out that it was necessary to pump the ship twice a day to keep water out of her bilges; three feet of ocean managed to seep in every twelve hours. Despite all the difficulties, by nightfall the decks were cleaned and the gear was in working order. The lofty peaks of the Andes faded into shadows as the sun dipped below the horizon where the sky blended with the sea in the west. Nothing was out of perspective or order—but the crew.

From the first day I did not care for the chief mate, a Chilean Spanish Indian. The second mate, a small blond Spaniard, was more to my liking. I felt that he and I could work together well, and we did. It was the job of the chief and second mate to choose the crewmen and classify them. They selected the harpooners first. Next they chose the helmsmen, the category into which I fell. There were eight men aboard who could steer a ship including Sam Vale, an old hand on a whaler. Traditionally the first mate headed the port watch and the second mate the starboard. I was assigned to starboard.

"Starboard watch," the second mate yelped, "go below until eight o'clock. I'll take the first dog watch."

This was the way it started, with the game little Spaniard carrying his weight all the way.

Now the work had ended for the day. It was nearly six o'clock in the evening, and the cook was yelling for all hands to stand in line at the galley door. He handed each of us a dish of bean soup, a piece of bread, and a pint of coffee made from burnt corn. It was not the kind of food served to sailors today.

When we had eaten, we went to the fo'c'sle to try for some order in bunk arrangements. This proved impossible, and I finally found myself being pushed into the rear of the fo'c'sle beside a latticework bulkhead that permitted the air from the ship's bilges and cargohold to escape. The companionway down to the fo'c'sle from the main deck had no door; the opening was there day and night, fair weather and foul.

Fresh water was rationed from day to day as we left Valparaiso—one pint a day for each man. That was our portion for both drinking and washing. Laundrying our clothes was out of the question with this ration. To meet the need of laundry the ship's management devised what to me was a repulsive plan. Two thirty-gallon barrels were lashed to the fore-peak deck forward; holes were bored in the top and spiggots inserted near the bottom. The men were instructed to urinate in the barrels and when the water for washing clothes was needed, to draw enough for that purpose. Some of us gringoes tried washing our clothes in salt water, but this proved impossible. Consequently we became as lousy as cuckoos. (The Latinos delighted in passing on their creeping things to us.)

65

One day Jim Ennis, the boy from North Dakota, rushed excitedly up to inform me that he had just seen the lubber from Argentina put a matchbox full of lice in my bunk. Old hand Jack Wilson said soberly, "Boys you are just too green for this kind of a ship. Look...I'll show you how to deal with these little varmints." He calmly removed his pants, turned them wrongside out, lighted a match and proceeded to burn the nits off the seams.

The time finally came when we had to face the urine barrels. Holding our noses with one hand, we drew the stinking stuff out and did our laundry. Surprisingly this proved to be the best compound for getting the clothes clean. It might have been called Operation Ammonia. After a vigorous rubbing, the garments were tied to a long rope and dragged through the seawater for an hour. Then we pulled them in, wrung them out, and tied them to the drying rope between the backstays. At last we had clean clothes...but the vermin in our bunks were still with us.

We did not get rid of the lice until we began to catch whale. When we saturated our clothing with whale oil, the lice disappeared. After that less laundry was necessary too. Toilet facilities were nil. We merely climbed to the jib boom braces and squatted like chickens on a roost.

After two days of sailing from Valparaiso, we took a course southwest by south and headed into the Antarctic Ocean with sperm whale our objective. Watchmen equipped with strong field glasses kept watch from daylight until dark on the fore and main mastheads. The harpooners repaired gear and sharpened harpoons, keeping nervously busy as they waited for the call of "B...L...O...W." For two months we sailed and sighted nothing. The old whalers, tense and expectant, grew increasingly anxious for a kill. About three o'clock one afternoon bedlam broke loose. The first "B...L...O...W" was bellowed from the mastheads.

Men jumped to their posts. I had been assigned to the second mate's boat crew. Our whaleboat hung in the davits on the starboard quarter, and two of us stood on deck to lower away while the second mate and our harpooner took up their positions at the stern and bow to lower the halyard. As the boat hit the water, three men slid down a rope into the whaleboat. The sea was rough. When we drifted past the stern of the ship, we lifted the portable mast into position and hoisted sail. Before lowering the boat, the second mate had taken bearings of the position of the beast and the direction of the wind. We set sail for this spot.

Within two miles we found him, a big sperm bull leisurely playing on the surface of the sea. As we came within two hundred yards of him, we lowered the sail and unshipped the mast. Quickly and noiselessly they were rolled and tied and stowed in one side of the boat; then we began to row directly toward the whale's broadside. With four long oars in that choppy sea, we headed for the kill. I could feel my heart pounding against my ribs as my muscles tensed and strained against the oars. It was clearly up to the oarsmen. I gritted my teeth and gave it all I had.

The whale was spouting streams of water mixed

67

with air that looked like a fountain. We were almost upon him, the misty spray falling upon us, when the order to retreat was yelled. We shipped around in our seats as the boat went astern. The mate yelled, "Strike!" The harpooner, Flores, black-bearded and more determined and accurate than his stature would indicate, sent the heavy harpoon straight to its mark. Maneuvering the boat according to the instructions of the mate, we watched the harpoon sink into the blubber of the left shoulder up to its iron shaft.

Rowing well away from the struggling beast, the mate took the harpooner's place, for it was a precedent that the mate must make the kill. The harpooner caught up the heavy steering oar, and with the crewmen on the oars we rowed forward and back as needed to maneuver the boat into position for the final kill. The mate held the diamond-shaped lance on the end of a four-foot iron rod attached to a wooden five-foot staff and awaited his opportunity.

The wounded whale made a dash for freedom, failed, and reared his great head high out of the water. I could see his little eyes on the sides of his head and his heavily toothed bottomed jaw opening and shutting like an enormous vice. The struggle continued for half an hour. We would succeed in getting into position to approach the struggling whale broadside, and he would thresh away from us. We dared not allow him to attack us head on with those jaws and their forty-two large teeth only four inches above the mouth's hard plating. And his flukes and tail were as dangerous as a battering ram.

Finally, after several thrusts of the long lance, the

whale began to spout streams of blood and we were literally baptized in it. His frantic efforts to get away lessened until the death run which measured about fifty yards. Now it was all over and the monster lay motionless on the surface of the choppy waters.

Quick action was necessary to prevent the lifeless form from sinking. Moving with alacrity despite his winding battle, the mate drove a harpoon with a rope attached to it into the blowholes located on the forepart of the head. This was fastened to the bow of the whaleboat. Another rope was passed around his tail and the carcass was allowed to sink about three feet. At this depth, it hung beneath the boat as we shifted the oars into the rowlocks and began the long journey through the dark back to the *Nautilus*.

We seemed to be rowing for hours. From time to time I glanced at the stars trying to determine time and to get my bearings in that wide expanse of sea. I had an eerie feeling of being lost between time-reckoning and eternity. The darkness thickened with the wind and the spray from the heavy sea washing around us. We toiled on, and I had the panicky sensation in the pit of my stomach that we were rowing for our very lives. At that moment it never occurred to me that it took super seamanship and cooperation on the part of all concerned to bring that whaleboat and its dead cargo into port.

After what seemed like a thousand years, the first mate's boat was able to contact us. It was actually about midnight when we received the end of a one hundred and twenty fathom towline to the ship. The ship hove to. We picked up the lee starboard side, and a heavy chain was swung from the bow of the ship. This chain was fastened around the tail of our catch; his head hung aft of the rudder and the rope attached to the harpoon in his blowhole kept his body near the sea's surface.

The first near-tragedy of the night's events happened then as our boat was hoisted and secured in the davits. Freed now of our own boat, we went to help the mate's boat on to the ship. A young Chilean seaman had been stationed in the stern of the boat to keep the double tackle running gear from fouling and twisting. The boat was about a fathom from the surface of the water when the bolt through the davit head gave way. With a loud crash of timber and a huge spray of water, the whaleboat fell back into the sea stern first.

The seaman lost his handhold on the hoisting gear and went headfirst into the turbulent waters. Consternation broke loose. The second mate sprang to the poop deck and fastened a life buoy to a long rope. The first mate and his crew lowered their boat immediately, and the quick action of both mates and their men resulted in getting the seaman out of the sea and back on ship.

All was not satisfactory regarding the prized whale which we had struggled to bring into the ship. As the wind increased in fury, the skipper decided to keep the ship hove to for the remainder of the night. He had an uneasy crew aboard as we listened to the cracking of the whale's moorings with every twist and jerk of the ocean's swell. Presently we heard a loud bang followed by the snapping of a chain which told us plainer than words that we had lost our first catch of the season. The boats were lowered and proddings for the huge carcass begun—but to no avail. These proddings lasted well into the next day, but the whale carcass had sunk immediately after being freed from its moorings.

There were those aboard who could not accept this without argument. There were all kinds of reasons brought up among the crew, chief among them being superstition. None could agree as to who the "Jonah" was. Some of the Latinos said it was because we had too many gringos on board and they were all for throwing us overboard with the whale. The second mate sat down on the hatch, put his head between his hands, and cried. It was his first catch of the season—his personal achievement. I shared his bereavement.

The old cliché that a bad beginning has a good ending proved true that season for us. After our initial disaster, we struck it rich in whales. The little second mate and his loyal boat crew killed fourteen, proving to the skeptical Latinos that he was not the "Jonah" after all. The other three boat crews got fourteen between them and brought the total to twenty-eight whales taken during the season.

Leaving the far south Pacific whaling grounds we headed north. In the next two months the men in the crow's nest sighted a few schools of sperm, and we captured six. On another occasion we were giving chase to a big bull when a school of hundreds of young whales surfaced all around us. They were so thick around our boats that we dared not make fast one animal. We simply sat in our boats while the monsters,

71

like frolicsome children, played around and beneath us.

After a whale was caught and brought back to the ship, the blubber had to be removed. This flensing processs had many facets. The starboard side of the ship was equipped with the necessary gear. There was a ten-foot movable gate in the bulwarks. A swinging scaffold attached to the ship's side was lowered for use, hanging three to four feet above the water. This scaffold was a plank about twelve inches wide with a hand guard around the inner side that would permit the crewmen to steady themselves as they worked.

Usually three men took up positions on the flensing scaffold, each one having a straight chisel-like hoe on the end of a ten-foot pole. The old winch with crossbar handles with room for ten men to work was on board. The main yardarm on the starboard side was tilted as high as it could possibly be raised. A heavy two-sheaf block was secured to the end of the yardarm, and a block the same size with a fathom of chain was placed at deck level. These pulley blocks were large enough to carry a two-inch rope with which the whale was secured to the ship both fore and aft. The men with the flensing spades (called *pill* in Spanish) took up their positions on the scaffold hanging just above the whale's body.

The fluke or fins were cut off and the chain from the tackle was fastened around the stub of the fluke. The winch began to lift as the flensing crew cut into the beef on the whale's body, and a sheet of blubber was cut or actually skinned off the carcass. There had to be two sets of hoisting tackle secured to the yardarm. As the great sheet of blubber was cut, it was hoisted aloft while the second tackle chain, fastened through two holes cut into the blubber close down to the body, lifted the free blubber from the carcass and swung it inward, lowering it to the deck. Crewmen hauled the blubber in and cut it up into strips suitable for handling with a pike or pick.

8

A pike was a four-foot piece of timber like a pick handle with a metal hook on one end. This was used for dragging these large pieces of blubber into the required positions. When enormous chunks of beef were hoisted indeck with the blubber, the knife men would separate the two. Much of this whale beef was cut into thin strips, cooked in boiling oil, and eaten by hungry workers. When well cooked it was quite edible. Nevertheless, I have seen great hunks of whale beef, often weighing as much as three hundred pounds, hauled to the gap in the bulwarks and slipped overboard, where they were instantly devoured by sharks. A shark would simply open his mouth and swallow the side of beef in one gulp.

The flensing system was halted after a couple of turns if the beast was a sperm whale. This was to allow the large head to be emptied. A door two feet wide and as long as needed was cut into the bony casement of the head. A block and tackle opened the door, and two men began to cut out chunks of pure sperm oil. As these were freed they were put into buckets and hoisted indeck where they were emptied into a big wooden tank with a capacity of two thousand gallons. The head oil was drinkable as it came out of the natural reservoir composed of small globules similar to those of a skinned orange. We frequently filled our pint pots with this warm oil and drank it.

After the blubber was removed it was cooked down

in a rendering process. The rendering or "trying out" works on deck were a simple arrangement. Two large metal cauldrons stood side by side on the main deck a few feet ab'aft the foremast. There was a cement and brick protection for the wooden decks, and the cauldrons stood on brick fireboxes. The blubber was cut into chunks, then sliced into thin flakes left attached at one end. A man with a pike could pick up a large lump of blubber held together at the edge. These pieces were thrown into the cauldrons with the heat provided by burning some of the crackling of a former boil. It was like rendering lard from hog fat. When the cracklings were brown and dry, they were ladled out to a dripping rack to be thrown into the fuel box for the next boil after they had dried. The white ashes were kept in a box and used as lye for scrubbing down the ship and paintwork when the season was over.

An unforeseen incident occurred later that took preeminence over the whaling with the captain. His wife became ill, and we headed for the Gulf of Guayaquil, Ecuador, to put her ashore. The men left on board, none of them exactly savory characters, became bored with inaction, and trouble broke out.

It began with a loud and lusty commotion coming from the officer's mess cabin. Most of the crew took cover in a hurry. I stood near the mainmast, my hand instinctively reaching out to grasp a twenty-nine-inch whalebone belaying pin. If I had to get into the fight, I planned to give a good account of myself.

The screaming and cursing ascended, and presently I saw the cabin boy being dragged on deck. He was

75

bleeding from the mouth and shrieking at the top of his lungs. The third mate followed him closely, kicking the helpless boy in the rear with every step. The guards dragged him to the starboard side of the deck and tied his hands together with rope. Then they moused his thumbs together with a piece of marlin rope to a quarter of an inch thick and hoisted him by the thumbs to the rigging of the mizen mast. There he hung—moaning, crying, writhing in agony with his toes dangling just above the deck. This sadistic cruelty was too much for me. I called the gringos together and begged them to take a stand.

"Arm yourselves with your sheath knives or any club you can find and let's go after them," I pleaded. One by one they turned their backs.

An older man muttered, "Nothin' doin'! He must be gettin' what is coming to him."

I appealed to Jim Ennis, the boy from North Dakota: "Will you follow me?"

"Just as well to go down like that as to die a thousand deaths through fear," he gritted in reply.

I shouted, "Let's go get the mate!"

We tightened our grips on our sheath knives and, armed with a stout belaying pin in the other hand, we went aft. I bellowed for the chief mate, who had started this. He came out cautiously and ascended the stairs slowly. Seeing our weapons he hastily held up his hands for peace, indicating a willingness to listen.

"Watch the skipper," I whispered to Jim.

"The skipper has a gun in his belt," Jim whispered back.

"Don't give him a chance to use it," I had time to

warn before the mate and skipper approached walking side by side to the main deck. I began to talk fast.

"Chief, no doubt you think you have to punish an offender, but look at that boy. He is unconscious, the blood streaming from his mouth. This is inhuman treatment. Cut him down right now"—I knew I had to make my words stick, so I edged up closer to the mate and prodded him with my knife—"or I'll spread your bloosy guts all over the deck!"

The mate moved away from the knife and looked at the skipper. They must have decided silently between them that they didn't want this kind of fight. The order was given to cut the boy down, and his bloody face and hands were bathed in clean water. We later learned that he had provoked this extreme punishment by drinking the captain's wine and refilling the bottle with water.

As Jim and I went for'ard, we talked it over. Both of us sensed that the battle was not yet over. The uneasy gringos trailed along protesting that they had been ready to jump into the fracas if needed. I turned to them angrily. "You damn cowardly curs," I yelled, "you let the two of us face them alone! But you'd better boot up your courage or you'll be next. We haven't heard the last of this yet."

The ominous quiet that followed the fight had the quality of a silence that proceeds a storm at sea. In it we sailed on as fast as the old packet would stand the wind; the objective of the captain now was to get his wife into port. With him this came before personal grievances.

We reached the Gulf of Guayaquil at the end of June

1911—a fact recorded in the ship's log along with the report that eight miles an hour was the fastest the *Nautilus* sailed on that run north. We dropped anchor in the Gulf five miles offshore, and the captain took his lovely wife and little son ashore in a whaleboat. The chief mate ferried them and remained away for two days.

As we fidgeted and waited we knew this absence was brewing trouble. We were right. When he returned the mate was drunk. Jim and I agreed to keep well out of his way.

When his liquor was gone, he had to have more. He loaded everything he could find that he could trade for booze into a boat—provisions from the ship's store, even essential equipment, and rowed it all to Guayaquil, this time returning with a supply of booze for the men. The drinking and fighting that followed were indescribable. Men lay drunk and bleeding on deck day and night. The captain had been away ten days, and the men were getting more and more restless. Some of the more wary wanted to get out of the mess. A faint whisper had been going the rounds for days about bolting or deserting the ship. This grew louder as the tension increased, and the plotters finally set a night to escape. The fourth mate was the originator of the scheme and thereby the leader of the half-crew forward that wanted to join him. Jim and I decided to go along with the escapees, although we were concerned about our chance of success.

It was midnight. The chief mate was in a drunken stupor in his cabin. Jim and I sat in the fo'c'sle head watching every move. The second mate—my favorite, if a seaman can have one—was on deck, watchful and alert. All evening the fights had been numerous, and men lay sprawled over the decks, amidship and aft.

The time for the escape had been set for ebb tide. The fourth mate would command his own whaleboat while the men slid down a rope into her as soon as she hit the water.

I whispered to Jim, "I'll go down below and put on another shirt and fill my tobacco pouch. If the fourth mate makes the slightest move, call me." I ran downstairs and struggled into my extra shirt.

Jim poked his head down the companionway. "Albert," he yelled, "they are going."

I bounded on deck, and we raced to the ship's side. The whaleboat was then past the ship's stern. I swore and would have jumped into the sea had not Jim grabbed my arm.

"No!" he said sensibly. "They will kill you before you can get into the boat."

Then I realized for the first time that bedlam had broken loose on deck. One glance in the dim light took in the situation. Officers with the still half-drunk and weaving first mate leading the way were coming from the cabin aft.

I nudged Jim. "Let's duck. They'll think we lowered that boat for the mutineers!"

We got below as fast as we could only to be summoned back by the loud call of the chief mate. "All men on deck!" he bellowed in a voice like a foghorn.

Perhaps our guilty consciences prodded us into reaching for our sheath knives as we slowly retraced our steps to the deck. Our baffled wits refused to take into account that he was merely wanting to check to see how many men were left. Slowly we replaced our sheath knives as he began to express his pleasure in seeing so many who had not tried to desert.

I was immediately chosen to accompany the second mate to go in pursuit of the mutineers. Preparation was noisy and short, but when I had the chance in the clatter to talk to Jim, I said, "If I don't come back with the crew, look for me three nights from tonight. I'll be prowling around the *Nautilus* in a rowboat to pick you up."

Jim held up three fingers to indicate that he had heard, and the tracking crew was off. The party consisted of two whaleboats with the now sobering first mate, the second mate, and two harpooners in the whaleboat I was steering. We set sail in the direction that we knew the wind and the ebb tide would take the escapees. It was still dark on the water; the wind was fair for a course northward along the coast. The first mate said he was positive they would head for the fishing village of Manti. He was right.

Our boat was light on the water; that of the fugitives would be down to the gunwales with fifteen men aboard. After about an hour's sailing, we saw a faint light on the face of the sea. A seaman had carelessly lighted a cigarette. This was the undoing of the escape venture. We steered a straight course toward the beach in front of the fishing village following that lighted match. To approach abreast their boat and attempt to board would have been suicide. These were shark-infested waters.

Daylight was breaking over the peaks of the Andes,

but the skyline was still dark. As we slowly came into the beach we could make out the shadowy figures of the fugitives beaching their craft. As yet they had not seen us. We quietly ran our boats up on the sand while they were collecting their gear. A man straightened and saw us. The group fled in panic, disappearing among the Indian shacks a hundred yards from the beach. The first mate and harpooners ran after them, shouting orders for the second mate who left me to guard the boats.

I waded and swam in the sandy bottomed surf while the second mate waited quietly on the beach. The sun arose over the Andes, chasing back the darkness and bringing to my mind poetry and philosophy I had not thought about in a long, long time. I could have escaped, but this morning I didn't want to. I looked from time to time across the waves at the still figure of the second mate, and suddenly there was an empathy between us. I thought of him whimsically as my "guardian angel."

I was getting experience in the school of hard knocks—an understanding of human relationships and the potential usefulness in all human life. And in my thinking backward and forward, a biblical quotation stashed somewhere in my subconscious—maybe a hangover from my childhood training—came to mind: "The wicked flee when no man pursueth; the righteous are as bold as lions." I knew then that I had no cause to flee. I could suffer hunger or injustice along with any man and come out the wiser for the experience.

This ended my time of peaceful thinking, for midmorning came quickly and with it the two harpooners and the first mate dragging one lone fugitive along with them. We hauled the empty boat up on the sand and left one guard over it. While we were thus engaged, the captors proceeded to beat the man they had captured. This accomplished, they threw him into a boat and we shoved off toward the mother ship which we reached early in the afternoon. Once on deck we were told to eat, then to return to the village for the other boat.

The third mate named three crewmen to return with me to pick up the boat we had previously abandoned on the beach of the Indian fishing village. This time when we landed a delegation of Equadorians was at the water's edge to welcome us. Friendly and full of questions, they offered goods and fruit for sale. I walked and talked among them, knowing full well that I could have disappeared into the crowd never to be found by a scouting party.

For a moment I considered it. The memory of the stark fare of the *Nautilus*—the beans, bread, and burned corn coffee—was vivid, but I squared my shoulders and did not look back toward the village. I remembered that I had no reason to flee; I would be like that biblical lion. I would come out of this experience on the *Nautilus* with an honorable discharge.

Back aboard ship everyone got busy cleaning up the mess. Blood and debris were all over the place. Fully sober now, the first mate went ashore to find the captain to inform him of the trouble. The crewman left on the dock to guard the boat while the first mate went ashore got drunk and drowned in two feet of water. We never learned the details. The mate and men did take time to bury him, although they grumbled at the delay.

Eventually the captain was located, and when he learned of his ship's plight, he began negotiations to round up a new crew. We needed fifteen men to replace the deserters and the man who had drowned. The task was not difficult, for at that time there were numerous shanghai-strong men in all west-coast ports. The captain contacted a German shanghai agent, and in five days we had fifteen Equadorian Indians aboard.

Most of these men were young, some possibly in their teens. Bruco, the exception, was perhaps fifty years old. All had their teeth filed like sharp saw teeth. Eating raw fish and whale meat was no problem to them.

While the new men were still eating, we lifted anchor and set sail for the Galapagos Islands. The second day out the mate undertook to initiate these inexperienced young men into the running gear of the ship. They did not engage in the whale chase; they were employed to do day-to-day ship work and to cut blubber. The young ones found no obstacle in going aloft, but the older man, Bruco, would not go into the ship's rigging above the gunwale.

83

9

No amount of inducing could persuade Bruco to climb to mainmast head. He merely stood stock-still and shook his head. The mate became so enraged at the man's attitude that he seized a dried sharkskin and began to beat the man about the head and shoulders.

The older man made no effort to fight back; he simply stood there on the rail weeping as blow after blow descended on his back and head. Then, as though at a given signal, the young Indians surrounded the mate with drawn sheath knives. There was no sound except the old man's sobbing and the mate's surprised and frightened cries as he began to plead for his life. Old Bruco got down from the rail, wiped his eyes, and quietly asked the boys to spare the mate's life. To me this was another lesson learned in loyalty to one's kind.

Around the Galapagos Islands we killed five more sperm. That accomplished, we headed for the humpback whaling grounds in the Gulf of Panama. There were some basic differences in these two kinds of whales. Because of the sperm whale's physical structure, he was rather slow moving in the water. This was due to his tank-like head, the short flukes, and the narrow spread of his tail. In contrast, the humpback whale was fast in the water with a head shaped like a giant frog's mouth, long flukes, and a widespread tail. The humpback was also classified as a baleen-bearing whale (a sucker and swallower) while the toothed sperm was a biter and chewer. The baleen in the humpback's mouth was like thin strips of plastic placed on edge all around the bottom jaw. He fed on plankton rather than fish.

It was the middle of August when we reached the humpback grounds. There we discovered that our hand harpoon and hand lance method of killing was impossible in water more than twenty fathoms deep. The humpback was too fast, and he swam in a spiral while feeding, then reversed, creating a current of swirling water. Obviously we had to change our methods.

The humpback came into the warm shallow water to calve* about the end of August; the calving and mating season lasted until the end of October. It was only in shallow water during the calving season that humpbacks could be harpooned at all. So in the Gulf of Panama we dropped anchor in a convenient channel between several small islands where the ship lay for weeks in the same spot. Each morning at daybreak two boats would be lowered to go in search of whale.

During the hunt we killed twenty-eight humpbacks; practically all of these had newborn or young calves. The calf was harpooned and held until the mother was killed, then turned loose with the harpoon still in its

---

*In giving birth to a calf, the mother would lie on the surface of the sea. The calf seemed to swim into view and immediately began to feel around for the mother's milk glands. A newly born whale calf is a beautiful thing to see. It is clean and smooth with little sightless eyes that shine like flashlights in the night.

back. A very small percentage of these calves lived. We killed the cows in the process of calving; the harpooned mother would not leave the calf until the death struggle set in. Even then, it was a flash of speed lasting only a few minutes. The calf still on the harpoon stayed with its mother's dead body until the carcass was towed to the factory ship.

The whaling crew had to learn the hazards of the sea as soon as possible and be prepared for any emergencies. Even then whaling was a dangerous business.

One morning we made fast a cow and a big calf and were settling down to the regular procedure for the kill when a huge bull surfaced near us, took the calf on his right fluke, and swam away with the cow and the calf. The ropes began to smoke through the lead grooves in the bow. We were holding a taut line, and the boat was thundering through the water with the gunwales six inches below the surface. Great curved waves rolled from our bows, and only our speed prevented us from being swamped. A tremendous plunge of the beasts forced us to give them rope. They surfaced and took our lines out of the boat. We held on until our hands were rope-burned, but to no avail. That was it for the day. We limped back to the ship with an empty boat and all of our gear gone. In this business, as in any other, there were good days and bad. This was one of the bad ones. Another day we harpooned a big bull that stove our boat in before we could subdue him. Even with the boat awash with water, we held on until he was dead. One good morning, we lowered the boat and went cruising near a small island where we found a cow giving birth to her calf. The harpooner hit her so accurately that she was dead with one thrust. We were back aboard the ship with the carcass at eight o'clock, our mission for the day accomplished.

About ten o'clock one morning we were cruising up toward Panama City when we sighted a blow between us and the waterfront. It was a long way off, but we got ready for it by taking out our Indian paddles. After a few minutes of paddling, the second mate said, "It's a singing bull. We'll wait a time and see if he blows again."

We could see the streetcars running on the Panama waterfront and hear dynamiting on the canal. The tropical sun burned down on our bare backs, and the sail hung motionless from the mast as we waited. Presently we felt the timbers of the boat vibrating, and as we put our paddles into the water, there seemed to be a whale concert coming from the depth of the sea.

"Forget about this fellow," the second mate said. "He is wild and too hard to handle."

As I listened to this lone concert chills went up and down my spine. He sounded like a lost soul in torment.* This hermaphrodite whale was a freak of nature. When mature he had been driven from the

---

*The sound might be approximated by filling a football field with a band equipped with every known kind of instrument—all being played at one time with no regard for harmony. (Fifty-five years later when I heard modern music with its weird discord, I was reminded of the first time I ever heard the bellowing of a hermaphrodite whale.)

87

herd because of his sexual abnormality. Thus he became an outcast to roam the oceans alone.

We sat very still, not wishing to frighten the beast by a movement of the paddles or a rap on the timber side of the boat. Sweat poured from our tanned bodies. We welcomed the rest from paddling.

Suddenly, without warning, the beast leaped to what seemed to be about thirty feet into the air a few fathoms in front of us. Three times he repeated this, then stood with his head in the water and his huge tail coming down in thunderous crashes on the surface of the water.

With the whale in this position, the second mate decided to try for the kill. "Straight ahead, boys, right at him with all the strength you've got," he shouted.

Quickly the sail was pulled taut in the light breeze, and paddling with all our might we approached that great uplifted tail. The mate yelled, "Strike!" The harpooner gritted his teeth and poised the harpoon for a deep thrust. The whale's tail was descending when the harpoon cut cleanly into his abdominal rear. Working swiftly and in unison, we lowered and stowed the sail and mast on the starboard side of the boat, then settled down in our positions for the kill. The second mate took the harpooner's place. The lances were readied, but we had to be closer to use them. To prevent the boat from being towed under, we had to give this mammoth fellow slack in the line.

This was his opportunity, and he took it. He headed straight for open sea. In vain we tried to come up to him when he surfaced so the lance could be used, but the harpoon was too close to his tail. The third mate's boat crew came toward us when they saw our helplessness. Their intention was to help, but they came at right angles. Misjudging their speed and distance they rammed us amidship and stove in our starboard gunwhale. With our own difficulty went the last chance to capture and kill the giant hermaphrodite whale.

September 30 came and with it my twentieth birthday. It fell on Sunday, and we arrived aboard ship at ten o'clock at night. We had killed a big humpback, but I felt no triumph—only a little sorrow that I was so far from home on my birthday.

We cruised expectantly around the emptying water without sighting a single beast. By mid-October we knew we had all we would capture for the season. Things moved swiftly after that. The first stop was at Guayaquil to take home our fifteen Indian members of the crew and to clean up ship. When the Indians had been paid off and ferried ashore, we lifted anchor and headed for Valparaiso, Chile. With fair weather, wind, and a ship that had been cleaned from stem to stern, there was little for the crew to do but watch the sharks, which were attracted by the oily smell. Occasionally we would run into great schools of tiger sharks.

The out-and-out break between the chief mate and me came abruptly to a climax one afternoon during this run. When I came from the wheel there was a chess game going on between my friend, Jim, and the carpenter. The rest of the crew were loafing on deck.

"I'm going below," I said to Jim. "If orders come from the chief mate, call me."

Jim nodded in reply and continued playing. I went below for about ten minutes. When I returned the peaceful scene had changed to one of violence. The crew had disappeared, and the air was filled with the cursing of the chief mate, who stood over Jim with a poised whalebone belaying pin. The pose of the mate and the cowering of my friend got to me instantly. I rushed in and shoved Jim aside.

"You damned dirty coward," I yelled at the chief. "All this voyage you've been spoiling for a fight with me. Now you've got it!"

"You want to fight?" he yelled back.

"No," I gritted at him between my teeth, "I don't want to fight, but you aren't going to beat up on anyone just because you want to either."

We stood glaring, breathing hard, measuring each other. At the same instant we both turned as though to walk away. Then the chief mate did exactly what I expected him to do. He whirled and struck out with what would have been a deadly blow had it reached my head. I whirled too, however, ducked, and warded off the blow with my left arm, driving out and connecting with his guts at the same time with my right. The fight moved in closer, and we both became tangled about the feet in the ropes around the main mast rail.

The rope tripped me up first, and I sat down hard on the deck. The mate sprawled across my knees with his face on the deck. I reached out for the back of his head and smashed his face on the deck again and again. At this point the third mate stepped in, caught me by the hair, and stretched me backward across the

90

main hatch coping. Then he struck me with the whalebone belaying pin across the eyes. The blood spurted, dimming my sight, and I released the mate. Now my friend, the second mate, got into the action. With surprising strength for one small of physique and quiet of manner, he lashed out at the third mate, sending all the fight out of him with one blow.

Still dashing blood from my eyes I lunged for the first mate and dragged him to the lower side of the bulwarks to take him overboard. I was positive I could handle him once I had him in the water. Again the second mate stepped in. But for his timely intervention at that precise moment I would probably have killed a man—something that I would have regretted all my life.

Just as we were going overboard, the second mate and one of the harpooners grabbed us both and hauled us back on deck. More angry than ever because my intent had been thwarted, I beat the first mate until he crumbled in a heap. I let him drop, and exhausted I staggered forward against the fo'c'sle head and dropped down in a heap myself.

The rest of the run to Valparaiso was without incident. We were a subdued and sober group; certainly we had a more reasonable chief mate among us. In Valparaiso I went to the shipping office for my pay. For eleven months on the whaling adventure, I received less than twenty-five dollars in U.S. currency. I had expected to get one hundred and fifty dollars, but I was told that we would not be paid off in full until the ship was unloaded and the oil measured. At that time this seemed reasonable to me.

Two weeks later I returned to the *Nautilus* to see if the rest of my money was available. Only the cook and the first mate were aboard. When the first mate saw me approaching the ship in a rowboat, he graciously lowered a rope. As I stepped on deck, he greeted me like a long-lost friend, giving me the *latino abraso* and insisting that I come to his cabin. Between his gestures of welcome and the opening of a bottle of wine with which we toasted the next year's catch, he explained that unloading operations were awaiting the return of the captain. Then he begged me to stick around and ship with him again, this time as his harpooner.

"Gracious, Señor, no," I replied. I was suspicious of his real intention, and my enthusiasm for whaling had been spent in the eleven months that had just ended.

I walked off the deck, went down the rope ladder to my rowboat, and left the *Nautilus* and her motley crew behind me. There was a glad feeling in my innards; my only regret was that I would probably never again see the second mate whom I had come to think of not only as a friend but as my guardian angel. If I never saw or heard of that hundred and twenty-five dollars I still had coming, at least I had not killed the first mate.

10

My next adventure began when I met a young Scotchman while I was walking on the waterfront in Valparaiso. I was looking for a job, he for men to hire.

"Can you do steeplejack work?" he inquired.

"If you mean climbing aloft on ships, chimneys, and buildings," I replied, "the answer is yes. I can go anywhere on rope or timber that will carry my weight."

"You are hired," he said giving me a straight look. I had a feeling that he thought I was bluffing, but I had not been reared in the tall timberlands of Australia without gaining something from it.

"You can go to work painting for me," he said, naming the location of the job. I was on the appointed spot at eight o'clock the next morning. An old Russian-Finn seaman was my only companion on the job. For six weeks we worked side by side painting huge gasometers. Most of the work was done from a swinging bos'n's chair high above the ground. As I painted, I kept a watchful eye on the harbor for ships that dropped anchor each day. There was a certain kind of ship I was waiting for—one flying a British flag. It finally sailed into port.

Before I went to work the next morning I got a boatman to row me out to the three masted full-rigger and, once there, I climbed up a rope ladder and stepped on deck. The first mate to whom I was directed was a Scotchman named McGregor. His first question was, "Do you speak Spanish?"

93

"I can talk and cuss in sailor language as well as any Latino you ever met," I boasted.

He looked me over sharply. "Then come aboard tomorrow mornin', lad. We are unloadin' general merchandise from Liverpool, and the damn thieves are carryin' it off as fast as we can unload it."

I went to my paint job and told my employer that I was going to sea with another Scotchman. He paid me in full, and I bought a few clothes. The next morning I reported for duty on the *Kensington*.

The work was more or less familiar. I was put in the ship's hold with the crewmen unpacking merchandise and loading it into cargo slings. These were hoisted out of the ship's hold by a steam donkey-winch, then loaded into lighters at the ship's side.

I soon developed a certain finesse with this unloading. The crewmen suspiciously eyed each crate, hefting it, even smelling it. When the contents were found to be English plum pudding or English fruitcake, the crates were handled tenderly, and the crates that ascended to the donkey-winch were several cakes or puddings lighter. Almost automatically the men loosened their belts to make room for the stolen delicacies kept behind. Here was temptation at my fingertips, and I was not one to avoid it. I had lived on beans, whale meat, and greasy crackers too long. I simply shared the stolen morsels with relish and kept my mouth shut. I suspected that First Mate McGregor knew that the thieving did not come from ashore.

As it turned out even thievery can have humorous quirks. A hand named Paddy had pushed aside a likely-looking crate for his own personal inspection later. About that time the mate was serving morning rum on deck. Not wanting to miss either of the goodies, Paddy gulped his rum so fast he almost strangled and scooted back to the hold to investigate his likely-looking box. When the rest of us returned a few minutes later, Paddy was swearing in all the languages at his command and a few more. The duplicity of merchants in shipping their wares was his target. "You'd think they'd be ashamed to ship out such paltry items as coffin mountings—and in silver too!" He hurriedly refastened the lid of the box that had held such promise.

Weeks passed, and eventually we were unloaded. Then we took on a return shipment of Argentina barley for the breweries in Hull, England. I was sent into the hold to supervise the stowing of the sacks. Here I discovered that the husky Chilano stevedores knew more about loading the ship than I.

One of the men we signed on before sailing was another Australian, Frank Hart. He had been whaling with the *Piscadora*, a sister ship to the *Nautilus*. Hart was an interesting man who had served several years with the British Navy. He was tall and thin, with white kinky hair framing his negroid-like face. He was frequently referred to as the "white nigger." Perhaps only I knew that he was a descendant of the famous Steve Hart family, notorious in the days of the Kelly Gang of Australian bushrangers.

The full-rigger *Kensington*, with an English-speaking crew, was paradise to me after my experience on the Spanish whaler. I hadn't realized how homesick I had become until we were actually under way and

95

homeward bound. I was probably the happiest of the seamen aboard.

We sailed about fifty-five degrees south, then turned east to round the Horn. The weather was cold and we encountered some snowstorms. The rigging became ice-clad and dangerous. Before we reached the Horn, we had strung lifelines shoulder high from the deckhouse forward to the poop deck aft. This assisted the seamen in passing along the deck they had to travel in pursuit of duties. The weather, however, did not dampen my enthusiasm for this voyage home. I began to plan what I would do when I got to England. I would get a ship and sail up the Baltic Sea to visit my grandfather who was living in Stockholm.

As we turned eastward, sail was shortened because of bad weather, and when we rounded the Horn, the seas coming off the Antarctic pounded our decks with terrific force. With reefed foresail and topsail on the foremast, reefed spanker and inner jib as our only sails, we held to a course and moved slowly into the gale winds that were buffeting us.

At ten p.m. I relieved Irish Paddy at the wheel. The course was south by east, full and by the wind. Because of the heavy seas, passing from one end of the ship to the other was possible only by holding on to the lifelines we had strung. At midnight Frank Hart came to relieve me at the wheel. With a feeling of relief I gave him the course.

"The wind is tricky, Frank, and the seas are heavy for handling the wheel," I said. "Watch her, eh?"

He repeated the course, took the wheel, and made no further comment. I saw the captain come up on the poop deck as I grabbed the lifeline and swung to the main deck. Groping my way forward and into the fo'c'sle, I was in the process of removing my oilskins and sea boots when the ship lurched to starboard. The sudden lurch sent me sliding under the bunks, and the horrible thought that the ship was capsizing raced through my mind. I heard the mate yelling, "All hands on deck, a-l-l hands on d-d-eck." He was shouting with such an urgency in his tones that I hurried back into my oilskins and out on deck.

All hell seemed to have broken loose. Men were running in every direction. The mate was struggling to get the fore upper topsail down, while other officers were frantically working to get the main and after gear in order. The mate grabbed me and yelled, "Loving, get aloft and ride that topsail yard down so we can make these sheets fast."

I went as quickly as I could in the terrific gale, stood on top of the upper topsail yard, took hold of the chain halyards, and pulled with all my might on the gear. The yard began to descend slowly as the men on deck hauled on the clew lines. Only then did I realize how near we had been to going down by being struck a'back by the winds and sea. We had sailed right into the eye of a hurricane. For the next six hours we took a terrible beating. When daylight came we were still working to get running gear cleared and the ship established on a course.

Ten o'clock the next morning we all huddled under the poop deck, thanking our Deliverer that we had come through the night. The mate brought out a bottle of rum, and almost reverently each man took his noggin. We were a subdued and weary group of men.

Eventually we resumed our regular watches and sailed on up the Atlantic coast of South America between the Faulkland Islands and the mainland and north across the Atlantic. We sailed into the English Channel, past Greenwich, and on to Hull which was on the Humber River. As the tugboat hauled us up the Humber River, we stripped the sails and running gear off the masts and stowed them in the sail locker. The ship looked like a ghost with bare spars as she silently glided to dock. It soon became evident why the mate had advised us to have our gear ready in our seabags to jump ashore as soon as we arrived at the docks in Hull. Immediately as the boat glided into dock the beachcombers swarmed aboard like rats. We got ashore as fast as we could.

My childhood desire had been fulfilled. I had dreamed of rounding the Horn in a windjammer, and I had done just that. Now I was ready to go home to Australia. I wanted to talk...maybe brag a little...to my father and his friend, the old Russian Finn, around the fireplace in my childhood home. Before I could do that, however, there were the details of disembarking and signing off.

Liverpool was my next stop. Some of the crew were traveling there by train together, for we had arranged with the Board of Trade to get our payoff at the Liverpool Sailors' Home. From the boat we took a bus to the railway station, and in a few hours we were in Liverpool. There again we were met by bus and taken to the Sailors' Home, convenient transportation which we had paid for from our checks.

98

In Liverpool I did little except to buy a new suit of clothes. I did, however, walk miles over the city to see what it had to offer. Soon I got itchy feet: I wanted to get on the Baltic Sea and visit Grandfather Andrew Peter Lofving. A berth on a fruit boat up the Mediterranean was offered me, however, so I decided to take that and backtrack to Stockholm later.

While I waited for the fruit boat a tall middle-aged man came into the Sailors' Home asking for seamen wishing to ship out to South Africa. I went to the desk at the shipping office and asked the clerk to give me my Board of Trade seaman's book. When he had done so, I turned to the inquiring mate of the three-masted barque and handed it to him. It was as easy as that to change my well-laid plans.

I met him at the shipping office in half an hour. There were close to fifty men assembled waiting for a chance to ship out on the barque to South Africa. The first officer was interviewing men as fast as he could call out names and reject or accept them. Presently he called my name and indicated that I was to be hired. I joined the others waiting to sign on in an adjoining room.

By ten o'clock the next day the chosen ones were aboard, and by midafternoon a tugboat took the *Amulree* in tow down the Mersey River and out to sea. The crew was busy bending sail and fixing running gear. The next day we sighted the Irish coast and headed east for South Africa.

At Port Durban we unloaded general merchandise and ran light to Deluga Bay in Portuguese East Africa where we discharged one thousand tons of pig iron

99

and took on the same amount of gravel for ballast. From there we headed out across the Indian Ocean for Australia. I was homeward bound at last!

The *Amulree* was a lovely little ship to handle. She carried a crew of eight A.B.'s and fourteen apprentice seamen. This pleasant voyage could easily have made a confirmed seadog out of me had it not been for the hand of destiny. Homesickness was overcoming me completely. By Christmas, when we arrived in New Castle, New South Wales, I withdrew my wages explaining that I wanted to visit my parents in Queensland. The Captain gave me a six-pound advance, and I dressed up in my best suit to walk ashore. I knew then that I would never see the *Amulree* and its congenial crew again.

11

On the train to Sydney where I was to meet my older brother, Cyrus, it began to dawn on me that I was living without intent or purpose. Adventure and experiences are not worth much, I told myself, unless they lead somewhere. A transition is the smooth flowing of one incident into another, but it is rarely true of life itself. The old adage, "Hindsight is better than foresight," began to assert its truth in my mind at this point. I wanted to go home to my father's farm home at Inverlaw, Queensland, to study and to think. I had had four years of the roughest sea life imaginable; now I wanted the time and opportunity to try to sort out the values that were important to me.

The restlessness and challenge were still on me as my brother and I worked at various jobs around Sydney. The companionship of my brother and the labors we were involved in did nothing to relieve the recurring memory of the experience I had had in the Andes mountains, however. I needed time and solitude to meditate...to try to find answers.

I quit my pointless wanderings and went home to Inverlaw. There I planned to spend a short time, ease my homesickness, and get caught up on news—in addition to sinking my teeth into some of my mother's good cooking. The "short time" grew into weeks as I delved into Father's old books, especially Corbett's *History of the Protestant Reformation*. From that I went to the Book of Mormon. I felt strongly that the

101

history of the forgotten peoples of both American continents must be contained within these pages, for certainly the truth of their civilization had not been found elsewhere.

At this time I felt there was no reason for being "different" unless that difference stood for human need or enlightenment. The aftermath of a few months of study and meditation was that I made up my mind to follow the star of my vision. If I could not find my answers to the jigsaw puzzle that held me in so tight a grip here, then I would take a ship and return to South America to follow the divine leading that had impressed me there four years earlier. My intellect told me that I could discover nothing with a spade alone. I had to know something of the culture and language that any explorations would reveal. I needed to study to be an archaeologist, for without knowledge and understanding the mysteries of the Book of Mormon world would never become an accepted historical fact.

Then the quiet life of my homeland got in my way and undermined my determination. What I needed at that particular crossroads of my life was for someone to say, "Go do it, Albert. Go help prove the divinity of the Book of Mormon and find the facts concerning its people." But no one said it. In fact most people thought me a little strange because my zest for truth led in this direction when their own was wholly caught up in converting every man they met to the idea of the Restoration—the pure gospel returned to earth by an angel.

Church leaders were not wholly to blame for their lack of vision. They were often zealous without

102

wisdom, but this was a new church and a new breed of men—mostly uneducated but honest, fired with the purpose of spreading the gospel to the utmost ends of the earth. This meant preaching the six fundamentals —the truths a candidate needed to acknowledge and adhere to to become a member. The time wasted arguing with their Utah cousins came in the matter of course as each got into the other's hair doctrinally.

Preaching and living the gospel took priority over everything else in my father's life. Our family, I'm sure, was a happier one because its members were guided and held together by certain bonds of teaching and love. The only thing not as well understood in that day was that many, many roads led to God, and that anything done in the name of Christ for the sake of humanity was a calling to good. This was the way I looked on my study of the Book of Mormon—a way to serve God and my fellowman that I would thoroughly enjoy and appreciate.

Then Apostle Gomer Griffiths came into my father's group of dedicated church people with a tremendous capacity for work and indefatigable powers of persuasion. Soon two young men—Angus McKay and H. I. Velt—were ordained to the office of priest. Then I too was called to take on priesthood responsibilities. The argument of my friends that I could continue my studies and yet serve as a priesthood member pleased me. Putting aside my misgivings, I yielded to what I thought was the greater wisdom of my superiors. I was ordained a priest at the reunion of the Queensland group at Inverlaw by Bishop George Lewis of New Castle.

I learned slowly that priesthood responsibilities encompass a lot more than serving in the way we wish to serve. Now instead of shipping back to South America to pursue my education I was made church school superintendent by the dictation of my superiors. At times, accompanied by other young church appointees, I visited farm homes and held cottage meetings. Early in my ministry I saw the advantage of this type of ministry.

Gradually, though not wholly reconciled, I warmed to what was expected of me. On one occasion I accompanied Elder Bryan Longfield to Kingaroy where we met two elders of the Utah church in a private debate. While I was personally convinced that the Reorganization had truth on its side, I was still not satisfied that I wanted to preach. If preaching also meant debating with other churches about what is right and what is wrong, I did not want to waste time that way. I wanted to study; I wanted to know if I was preaching truth. I remembered that William Booth, founder of the Salvation Army, had once said, "Tell the truth though the heavens may fall."

In retrospect I realized that I responded to the pressure of so-called inspiration. Elders and friends were the deciding factor in my becoming a missionary. These well-intending men did not realize that they were pushing me into a life's choice of vocation. Be that as it may, I finally submitted to their counsel. I was ordained a priest and sent out to preach the word of God as a missionary. When I did so I accepted their leadership, and as one door opened before, another closed. I followed—sometimes I'm afraid almost blindly—down a pathway that was guided by the hierarchy of the church, a guidance that was to be the main stimulus of my activities for the next forty years. Shuttled now to the background of my interests lay my longing to study linguistics and archaeology.

Elder Walter J. Haworth was at that time acting minister in charge of the Australian Mission, and I was sent to work in the Victoria District. J. H. N. Jones was president of that district, and I was happy working with him. We had a great deal in common; he knew much about ships and had at one time been a commercial fisherman. I learned a lot while working with him in Victoria District. Later we worked together in the New Zealand Mission.

Groups and branches had been established at Hastings, Glen Forbes, and Phillips Islands. There were church members in all of these locations who had been baptized by the early missionaries of the Reorganization. At that time we knew as little about church history up to the period of 1844 in Nauvoo, Illinois, as we knew about the Book of Mormon. New Testament Christianity with the gifts of the Holy Ghost was the foundation for all missionary work in Australia. Prophecy, tongues, the interpretation of tongues, healing, and knowledge were common expressions of spiritual life in our meetings. I was a little impatient with those who stressed these outward manifestations, but I did hunger for a knowledge of God and the truth concerning what was called the Restoration. Accepting the divine gifts but not dwelling on them, I bent my talents toward a search to know God and his purpose for mankind.

An institution cannot very successfully detach itself from its historical roots. As most observing people know, the public looks mostly at the exterior of religious activities. The preacher who can put on the best show becomes a public idol. Before going to work in the Victoria District in 1916 I served for a few months in the Queensland District where my associate was a very young elder, Herman Peisker, ordained at the age of nineteen and elected district president. All his family had come out of the Utah church into the Reorganization some years earlier. During my association with him I studied extensively but did little preaching, and only a couple hours each day were devoted to personal contact work.

We had been in the South Burnett area of the state in a railroad town named Wondai from which we went to the city of Maryborough on the coast. In this city were a few already converted members including a Swedish family named Olsen. The demands for ministry were stepped up considerably by the good people of this region, and it did not take me long to realize that I had nothing to offer in administering the plan of salvation to those in need. I simply did not know enough about it myself.

I was troubled by this inadequacy, yet there was nothing I could do but keep my fears and misgivings to myself. Eventually I decided to resign from the missionary arm of the church, return to Peru, and study archaeology.

As was my custom, I took my concern to a session of private prayer as I got ready to retire for the night. I told the Lord that surely someone had made a mistake in appointing me a missionary and that I was going to send my resignation to the minister in charge. My mind was made up, I reminded the Lord, as I argued that there were better qualified men than I to preach. I went to bed and slept well. During the night, however, I had a vision. I saw a number of immortals—"just men made perfect"—standing around my room engaged in conversation about Herman Peisker and me. I sat up in bed and spoke aloud, "Why are you immortal beings gazing on us?"

As I uttered these words the vision vanished, and I lay back down on the bed. I was awake but lay with my eyes closed when there appeared before me an open Bible, and I could see across the top of the page the word "Timothy." As I read down the page the letters seemed to stand out in bold black type.

The next morning I took the Bible and read Paul's letter to Timothy. I was curious to see if the words I had seen were there. They were.

The pillar and ground of the truth is (and without controversy, great is the mystery of godliness,) God was manifest in the flesh, justified in the Spirit, seen of angels, preached unto the Gentiles, believed on in the world, received up into glory. —I Timothy 3:16.

To scoffers, I had the truths on which to work. I had seen immortal beings, and I had seen an open Bible. I had a personal testimony. I knew then, as I know now, that Jesus Christ was God in the flesh. My mission was to teach this truth to my fellowmen. My doubtings concerning my calling were gone.

During the time of my work in the Victoria District a few people were baptized in the sea on Phillip

Island, and I did some preaching in the church at Hastings, a fishing village on the bay. Some old-time members of the church were Ashton Wooley, Max Kippe, the Graydens, the Baxters, and the Bowes. Max Kippe was a convert to the Restoration at Hastings. He began immediately writing to his brother in Berlin, Germany. The result of this missionary work by correspondence was that Alexander Kippe joined the Utah branch of the church as he did not know the difference between it and the Reorganization. When Max learned what had happened, he took his two oldest sons with him to Berlin in an effort to extradite his misinformed brother from his error. He was successful.

General church headquarters at that time were in Lamoni, Iowa, and elders were dispatched to Berlin to baptize Alexander Kippe, who later became an elder and the church's official translator for years in a German mission.

The year 1916 found the entire country of Australia aflame with anti-German hatred. German people and aliens living there endured a great persecution; some were jailed. Max Kippe was no exception. One night in a dream I was in conversation with Max and his good wife when the word of the Lord came upon me, and I was instructed to say to them, "Fear not. Be thou faithful and trust in the Lord, thy God, and thou shalt not be moved out of thy house." This proved to be true. Hatred and prejudice and ignorance flowed around them, but the Kippes were allowed to remain in their own home.

We had no compulsory draft or military system in

Australia during World War I. In general, a young man looked upon conscription as an insult to his loyalty. "One volunteer is worth ten conscripts," was a familiar British phrase.

It was not long before Harold I. Velt, my missionary companion at this time in Bairnsdale on the Mitchell River in Gippsland, and I began to experience lifted eyebrows and insinuations about the fact that two able-bodied young men representing an American church were not taking their place in the Australian Army. Finding the social barriers hard to overcome, I presented myself at the recruiting office in the town of Sale and enlisted. This, however, brought a torrent of criticism upon me from some of the people of the church in Australia. Most of the members of the church at that time maintained an extreme isolationist attitude. To clarify my position, I appealed to the president of the church, Dr. Frederick M. Smith, about my action of enlisting. He replied in a kindly and understanding manner, commending me for loyalty to my government and wishing me well. His viewpoint quieted my misgivings at that time, though individual isolationists continued to feel that it could not be truthfully said that this opinion stemmed from leadership at headquarters in Independence, Missouri.

I got no farther than the physical examination for the army anyway. A gunshot injury to my right eye in my youth rendered me incapable of passing the eye test. Classified as a reserve to be called up when needed, I went back to my preaching.

12

It was while I was working in Bairnsdale that I met my future wife—Hilda Velt, a sister of Harold I. Velt, my missionary companion in Gippsland. The meeting came about naturally, since our mutual interests and faith attracted us to each other. Hilda was what was then called a "telephonist" and had been transferred from the Melbourne to the Bairnsdale exchange. But Miss Hilda Cecelia Velt was more than a mere telephonist. She was fired with missionary zeal and witnessed to the truth of the Restoration in a way that made many converts to the faith. One such converted youth was a lanky, red-haired messenger boy who worked out of the Bairnsdale post office. I helped in instructing this young man concerning the beliefs and practices of the church, and I baptized him along with several others in the Mitchell River. Later, he was ordained a priest.*

Hilda and I were married at her parents' home in Lower Bendoc, Victoria, August 31, 1917, with her brother, Harold, officiating. Our first child, Ethel, was born on August 12, 1918, in Bairnsdale. When Ethel was about three weeks old, we took her to the church service in Mechanics Hall (also called Temperance Hall) where she was blessed. I participated in this ordinance and, as the ceremony

---

*I mention this particular young man here because he seemed to be destined to figure prominently in my church life many years later.

proceeded, I had a strong impression that this child's adult life would be lived among people of the Latin American race. I also felt that she would not fully respond to the wishes of her parents.

Toward the close of 1920 Apostles Paul M. Hanson and John Rushton transferred me and my family to the New Zealand Mission where I relieved Elder Hinman W. Savage who had served there for eight years. By this time Harold Velt had been sent to Adelaide, South Australia.

Before leaving for my new appointment, I placed the red-haired Australian I had baptized earlier in charge of the church school in Bairnsdale. He became involved in Boy Scout work in Bairnsdale and Melbourne; later, as a scoutmaster in Victoria, he was selected to attend the Scout Jamboree in Denmark. He became such a favorite with the apostles that they arranged for him to come to the United States and attend Graceland College. After graduation this winsome Australian married a fine, intelligent woman some years his senior. Eventually he was ordained a member of the Council of Twelve.

Meanwhile, my wife, daughter, and I went by steamship from Melbourne to Dunedin to what was known as Christchurch and Wellington. We stayed a few days in the home of Elder Robert Hall before proceeding on to our ultimate destination, Auckland.

Mission headquarters were at 91 Eden Terrace in Auckland, and because of the difficulties in arrivals and departures, three different families lived in the mission house for a time. Here arose one of the problems in communal living. Before our arrival

111

Elders Savage and Robinson and their families had established the custom of each appointee putting a certain sum of money per week into a commonstock kitchen bag that hung on the dining room wall. Hilda and I were reluctant to concede to this type of arrangement, and we had a reason for our feelings in the matter.

The American family had two children, the Australians three children, and we had one—yet all of us shared an equal cost of living. My wife and I were of hearty pioneer stock and our dietary preferences were based on products of the land—beef, vegetables, and fruits. The other families had different tastes. This would not create a crisis today because a great variety of food is easily available, but it presented some problems then that required a lot of self-discipline to overcome. The old cliché that "no house is large enough for two families" was intensified here where the space was limited and differences were multiplied by three. We managed to get by, however.

I found that Hinman Savage was an excellent linguist in two of the Polynesian tongues. He had ministered on both the islands of Tahiti and Paumutu and was equally familiar with both languages. For this reason the apostles in charge, Hanson and Rushton, advised him to stay on in New Zealand to initiate me into the work among the Maori people. I must admit that I was not interested in this at first, but it began to grow on me. I found the people and their needs very fascinating and challenging.

Another phase of spreading the gospel in Auckland did not meet with my wholehearted approval either.

For several years prior to my appointment there, the major efforts of Elders Savage and Robinson had been preaching at the foot of Queen Street on the waterfront. I had done some street preaching in Australia, but in Auckland it seemed more damaging than helpful to our cause. The meeting place at the foot of Queen Street was like Hyde Park in Sydney. The spot was occupied every Sunday from two p.m. to ten p.m. by relays of representatives of different churches, cults, or political parties; consequently, what should have had the dignity of a service for Jesus Christ turned into little more than a performance for seekers of entertainment.

We had our turn each Sunday afternoon from four to six. In these meetings it was usual for members of the Rationalist Association to heckle every speaker with questions, objections, and insults. Our appointees spent most of the week studying in an effort to counter the criticisms of the hecklers. A favorite tactic of the Rationalists was to drag out the skeletons of Mormonism. We had to bear in mind that the Utah church had been well established in New Zealand for over fifty years. They had influential members in the government as well as in the Maori Agricultural College at Hawks Bay. The preaching of the gospel of Jesus Christ became a farce with futile debating between our appointees, the Rationalists, and representatives of other churches.

Practically all large Australian and New Zealand cities had this kind of forum where anyone who had a piece to speak could get a permit and an appointed place from the police. The custom also prevailed that anyone listening who disagreed or wanted to break up the meeting could interrupt with questions or get the attention of the speaker in any manner he chose. To me this was a degrading way in which to present the gospel of Jesus Christ; consequently, when the opportunity came to get out of the city and begin another type of ministry, my wife and I accepted our escape gladly.

In 1921 we went to the town of Rotorua toward the Urewera country with a good railroad leading to most of the important parts of the North Island. Here we bought a lot and built a small house on Elizabeth Street. The Te Arawa Maori tribe occupied this part of the island, and we knew that if we were to make any progress among these people we would have to learn their language. Many of them lived along the railroad tracks in King Country. Elder Savage and I visited them in their own habitat, and he preached to them in their native tongue. We also talked to them informally wherever we found them. Thus I was catapulted into missionary work among people of the Polynesian race. As I look back on those years in New Zealand, I am amazed that one so unprepared would be assigned to so important a task; yet I must admit that it worked to my learning advantage.

Confronted with Utah Mormonism on all sides, I decided to go to the root of each matter and dig out the truth for myself. I dared not depend on the opinion of others or their interpretation of history. Learning for myself was the only method that would work for me. The institutions of Catholicism and Protestantism were well established with literature, schools, and up-to-date facilities, but our message was unique, and in this babel of religious voices it began to make itself heard. The thorn in our flesh, so to speak, was Utah Mormonism. We were spending, and I felt wasting, much time in debating and explaining points of that doctrine which we regarded as false and without biblical authorization.

In the fall of 1922 Elder Savage and I attended a mission conference held by the Mormons at Huntley, a coal mining town on the Waikato River. We went there by train from Rotorua; en route we met many Maori passengers also going to the conference. These unprejudiced, sincere, delightsome people listened gladly to our story of the Reorganization.

On our arrival in Huntley Elder Savage and I secured rooms for three nights in a boardinghouse. We then went to the chief of police, identified ourselves, and obtained permits to hold meetings the evenings we would be there. The Utah people had engaged the town hall for dancing each evening, and we had our police permit to hold our meetings on the street in front of the hall.

Having laid the groundwork for presenting our side of the question, we went over the river to the spot where the Mormon conference was in progress. Once there, we simply mingled with the people, and many came and spoke kindly to us.

The president of the mission, John Taylor, did not choose to be charitable, however. He angrily reminded us that this was his conference and forbade us to talk with the people. When they saw us playing dumb because we had been forbidden to speak, they

115

began to look askant at President Taylor. When some of his own members went to him and demanded to know why we had been told not to speak, a problem he had not anticipated arose.

Each night we went to our spot in front of the town hall at the appointed time and preached until two o'clock in the morning. This went on all day Friday, Saturday, and Sunday. It came to a climax Sunday afternoon when the Mormon Apostle David O. McKay* preached. He said decisively, "Thus Mormonism and all it stands for today is the result of what God gave to the boy prophet, Joseph Smith."

Youth is often impetuous, and I was young and indignant. I jumped to my feet and in a clear, strong voice challenged him. "Mr. Speaker, I challenge that statement. The doctrine of polygamy was not given to the world by the boy prophet, Joseph Smith."

Having had my say I sat down, but I did not sit for long. I was immediately seized by as many hands as could fasten themselves upon me and dragged from the meeting to the road. There I was beaten and might have been killed had not a small group of Scotch coal miners jumped into the melee and saved my life. Even this did not abate my enthusiasm. I rejoined Brother Savage in carrying the argument forward in Huntley until past two o'clock the next morning.

Later that day Elder Savage went to Auckland by train while I began the return trip to my home at Rotorua. I learned, however, that leaving the scene did not end the conflict. A number of Mormon elders

---

*Later president of the Mormon church.

116

began baiting me, but they did not molest me. I soon learned why. As I left the train at Hamilton a man stepped out of the crowd and said, "I think you will be safe from here to Rotorua. Most of these fellows will be going on in this train." Only then did I learn that he was a plainclothes policeman who had been deputized to see me safely through until I was on the train to Rotorua.

A change of policy regarding our own ministry to the Maori people came about gradually. Elder Savage and his family returned to the United States while the Robinsons went back to Australia. Evangelist J. H. N. Jones was sent from Melbourne to work with me in Auckland. I had served agreeably and profitably with him before, and I was pleased with his coming. We abandoned the unprofitable street preaching and debating and concentrated on cottage meetings. This resulted in bringing the message of the Restoration and subsequently the Reorganization into the homes of people who honestly wanted to hear and be taught. Results of this change of policy soon began to be apparent not only in greater attendance at regular meetings but also in increased membership.

On March 20, 1923, our son Paul was born in the little cottage we had built on Elizabeth Street. Later in the year we sold the Rotorua house and moved to Copu in the Thames River Valley. Here we were in direct contact with the Maoris and had a few prospects among the whites.

While the four of us were living in a small apartment at Copu my brother, Cyrus, and his wife, Gertie, came from Queensland to seek employment.

Gertie, a very efficient schoolteacher, immediately made application to the Education Department of the Thames Valley for the position of director of schools at Kerepehi, a small town in the center of the Hauraki Plains. With this position, which she easily obtained, went a school residence into which they moved. Cyrus found work with a logging camp up Waiho Creek. My wife and I were heartened and supported by their arrival and loyal backing.

This area of the valley of the Thames was old Utah Mormon stomping ground, and we received opposition at every turn. One such incident was a four-night debate in a public hall in Copu with Sid Ensor, a local Mormon elder and member of the Thames city council. One of his chief arguments was that polygamy was necessary in order to fill the world quickly with people and thus prepare it for the second coming of Christ. Possibly on the basis of his oratory he was later elected mayor of the city. Today, in view of the population explosion, I am a little amused when I think of his claims. And the coming of Christ is not yet.

13

Interest in the Restoration church began to develop up the Piako River at a place called Tahuna. In rainy season this valley was more or less a swamp with small water courses intersecting it. The drier land was used for farming and grazing, while the main swamp was peat moss. A group of Mormon families were camped near Tahuna doing some large contract jobs of drainage and bridge building. They had a temporary meetinghouse in which they held services on Sundays. I walked to the meetinghouse one Sunday afternoon and, in customary friendly Maori fashion, was escorted into the building and given a seat. Services for the day had closed, and the people were sitting around talking and enjoying themselves.

I saw some hymnals on the desk with *Songs of Zion,* on the cover. I picked one up and asked, "Do you sing the songs of Zion?"

"Yes," was the answer.

"What and where is Zion?" I asked.

Several members looked at one another in puzzlement, then one man replied, "Zion is in Utah."

I picked up their Doctrine and Covenants and asked them to show me where in the book Utah had ever been called Zion. They merely continued to exchange glances, but had no answer.

About dusk the meeting place was visited by a small group of people and their chief, an old Maori named Pohutehuto. He was leader of the "Hau Hau, Rinnga tu" (big wind, hands up) group. In the process of their worship they would sit motionless in concentration until the big wind (Holy Spirit) moved an individual, who would then raise his hand indicating that he desired to speak.

The Maori Mormon elders asked that I engage the old man in a discussion on the subject of baptism for the remission of sins, probably because they realized that on this one point our two churches agreed.

After a few questions and answers, I proceeded to relate the biblical story of Philip and the eunuch, explaining in Maori language that Philip was sent by an angel of God to Gaza to find and talk to the eunuch about Jesus Christ. I put particular emphasis on the fact that Philip had been sent by an angel of God. Old Pohutohuto listened respectfully until I had finished. Then he said simply, "That Philip made a serious mistake in baptizing the eunuch. The angel that sent him also made a bad mistake."

From 1920 to 1928 when Hilda and I were working in New Zealand we came in contact with Ratana, a native religion. This movement began in a strange way. The man who started it lived in the village of Ratana. He reputedly was addicted to strong drink and had in his home a young daughter who was hopelessly crippled. One entire weekend the father had been drunk. His alleged awakening came when, upon sobering up to face his problem, he repented of his neglect of his child. He sought God in prayer on her behalf with the result that she was healed.

The grateful father began to relate the story of his experiences, and there grew up around him consider-

120

able interest in his powers of healing. Sick people came to him to ask for prayer, and he went about holding meetings for healing the Maoris. His fame as a healer spread even to include the sick of different faiths. He established a community at the village of Ratana and organized a church with twelve apostles and representatives to carry the message to interested people.

It soon became apparent that I had to have an answer to the question frequenly put to me by the Maoris: "Ahoa [friend], what do you think of this Ratana?"

It had become a matter of great interest to them regardless of the particular faith they had embraced. My first reply was to dismiss these happenings with a meaningless phrase, as one might answer a child, "Am I supposed to know?" But as the question continued to be directed to me, I began to realize that these sincere people were not going to be put off with such a reply to their honest question. I prayed over the matter and searched the Scriptures. I found my answer in the very words of Christ: "Let them alone. If they are not against us, they are for us."

"If Ratana's work is of God," I said, "I don't want to be found fighting it. If it is not of God, it will come to naught without me fighting against it." And they were satisfied with this answer.

In 1924 we had no literature in the Maori language, and I was the only missionary of the RLDS Church who was studying it in an effort to meet their needs. One rainy day I went to the home of a Utah Mormon convert named George. A very ill man named Cooney who had been converted and ordained in the Mormon church, but who now seemed to be doubting, lived with the family. The woman of the house told me that I could find the men in the barn husking corn. I went to the barn and began to talk about the Reorganization and the work of the first missionaries in the South Sea Islands and Australia dating back to 1883.

The sick man, Cooney, sat spellbound drinking in every word but saying nothing. And when I paused to give either of them the opportunity to comment or ask questions, George lifted his face from his work and said in stern Maori, "Very good, Mr. Loving, but where were your men of the Reorganization fifty years ago? At that time our ancestors listened to the Utah Mormon elders. They joined that church believing it to be the church of the Restoration. We have followed them in the same church. Now you come to tell us that the Reorganization is the continuation of the church organized by Joseph Smith in 1830. What is to become of our fathers? Why did you wait fifty years to come with the truth? And what will we do with the next one who comes with a different story?"

He had me there. I sat with bowed head and silently asked God to supply the answer in such a way that these men would understand. Then the sick man, Cooney, sat up and began to speak in excellent Maori.

"George," he said, "if Elder Loving had come fifty years ago, he would not have met you. He couldn't come before he was born, could he?" He continued reasoning. "Elder Loving is here now, and I know he tells the truth to all of us. Why don't you be sensible and listen to him?"

That was a direct answer from God and, since I could not improve upon it, I said no more. Presently, we arose and walked out into the fast approaching darkness. Cooney walked with me to the road, then told me that he believed in our message. He added that he was going to die in a short while and that he was glad to have heard the story of the Reorganization while he was yet in the flesh.

If he had asked for baptism I would have complied, but he did not. His mind was on other things—enlightenment for those who would be left behind with his passing. He told me of his friend, Waipapa Mangakahia, once a Mormon convert and now a member of the Catholic church, who lived at Whangapoua Bay. At one time he had been a licensed court interpreter. Cooney ended with the assurance that this friend of his would help me translate literature to clarify the Mormon question. I reluctantly left Cooney in the darkness and never saw him again. He died a few days later.

Following this incident, I set off for Whangapoua Bay on the east coast. I had to go through part of the Gulf of Hauraki lowlands and cross Cape Coromandel through thick jungle to get down to the bay (there were only cattle trails to travel, no roads). On top of the Cape mountain range with a clear blue sky above, I walked and meditated on my mission. A voice spoke from the blue of heaven saying, "Exploit the truths of the Book of Mormon."

Late that night I groped my way through fields and pastures and knocked on Waipapa Mangakahia's door. With native friendliness he opened his home to me.

Food was set before me—raw shellfish, boiled potatoes, and black tea. Then we sat down at a table and went right to work translating. The next morning we paused for a bit of breakfast, then resumed our work. After two days and two nights with him I walked to Thames on another trail with the translation of a tract in my pocket.

The tract we translated was one of the Angel Message series entitled *Was Joseph Smith a Polygamist?* Our manner of working was to go through the tract and number it off in paragraphs, then translate each paragraph separately. Mangakahia's knowledge of grammar and pronunciation was very good, and I had a fair vocabulary. We made good progress until we came to the last paragraphs. Here we disagreed over the conversation between Joseph Smith and William Marks. It was stated that Joseph Smith said, "Brother Marks, for a long time I have wanted to have a conversation with you on the question of polygamy. I will prefer charges against the men practicing it. I want you to go into the high council and, if they will not renounce it, I want you to expel them from the church." This conversation reputedly took place a short time before Joseph and Hyrum Smith were assassinated. There were facets of these statements on which my interpreter and I did not agree. I began to suspect that it depended on what we wanted to read into it. Mangakahia believed that polygamy was being practiced at Nauvoo and that Joseph Smith felt if it could not be stamped out the church would be forced to leave the United States. The question raised by the

Mormons was, "Was Joseph Smith thinking only of the probability of being forced out of the United States, or was he repentant?" These were the arguments advanced by Mangakahia who had studied in the Mormon church and had learned this interpretation in support of polygamy. I was anxious to refute the doctrine, because I believed with all my heart the thing that I wanted to believe—that Joseph Smith was trying to stamp out an evil that had crept insidiously into the church during his leadership. I had to work hard to get Mangakahia to translate according to my understanding. He resented changing his viewpoint but finally conceded.

Apostles Myron A. McConley and Clyde Ellis were now in Australia in charge of the mission. Accompanied by my wife and two children, I went to the April conference held in the old church at Balmain, Sydney. Here two incidents occurred that shaped my ministry. I was ordained a seventy, and I returned to New Zealand to take up the Maori work.

Before Brother Hinman Savage had returned to the United States he and I had worked on the Reporoa Plains in the center of the island with the result that a man and woman had been baptized, so we continued to study with and minister to them. My ministry had been in the Thames Valley where my brother, Cyrus, and his wife lived. Within the next three years a branch began to take shape at Kerepehi. Several newly arrived English families had been baptized, and some Maori people had received the gospel message. At Kerepehi I officiated in an unusual type of baptism service. One of our prospects was Bill Herkt, an

125

engineer, in the employ of the government. He also owned and operated a movie house in the village. He had attended our meetings and seemed to be converted, but remained aloof—probably afraid of public opinion. We told him that a private service could be arranged then left it entirely up to him, feeling that he would commit himself when ready.

In my spare time I was building a small house, and I needed sand and gravel which could be had only from an island in the middle of the Waiho River. I had to take my sacks in a scow from the bridge to the island, a distance of about three miles. I would fill them, load them into the scow, and row back to the bridge. From there a dray or truck would haul the sacks to my brother's house. The morning I started for the island, Bill Herkt offered to accompany me. Very pleased with his offer of help I set off with him for the island. We had filled our sacks and had them loaded into the scow when Bill said abruptly, "It is nice and quiet here. Why can't I be baptized now?"

We stripped down to our undershorts; then I offered prayer and led him into the water and baptized him. He was confirmed the following Sunday at a church service in my brother's home. A few months later his wife and three children were baptized. Later he was ordained an elder and proved a faithful supporter.

After the 1924 conference in Sydney, Apostle McConley came to New Zealand with the news that generous-hearted brethren in Australia had loaned the church sufficient money to build a mission house in Auckland. Bishop George Lewis came with the apostle to assist in buying a lot and erecting a building.

126

14

Soon after Apostle McConley, Bishop George Lewis, and J. H. N. Jones arrived in Auckland, a lot at 42 Leslie Avenue, Morningside, was purchased. It was a rock pile covered with a prickly plant about four feet high called "gorse." I was requested to come to Auckland to help with clearing the land and erecting the building.

A man named Davis from Tauranga and his son, Jimmy, were employed to begin the construction project. They remained until the frame building was up, then Brother Jones and I did the finishing. When it was ready for occupancy my family moved into one of the residential sections while the Joneses and their daughter, Phyllis, took the other side. Now we had adequate housing and a good meeting place. The church was beginning to take on a permanent status.

The organization of the Auckland branch, which had heretofore been a mission, proved problematical. Elder A. V. Robinson, stationed at Auckland, was regarded as specifically responsible for the activities there. Elder Savage was in charge of the entire dominion, while I was concentrating on getting the work started among the Maoris.

A well-known church man with worldwide business connections came to Auckland about this time on one of his periodic trips. He had the custom of attending to his business from his hotel room each morning, then taking a taxi and going about visiting church members in the afternoons. Sometimes, if I was in the city, he would phone me and request that I come to his hotel suite and assist him in decoding his cablegrams. This finished, we would go to dinner and then "priesthood visiting."

While Brother Savage was out preaching and teaching, this businessman got the idea of organizing the Auckland mission into a branch. As I have previously stated, Elder Robinson and I had had differences of opinion regarding the street meetings each Sunday afternoon. This "bull ring" session was Elder Robinson's baby, and he was inclined to insist on continuing it. On the matter of branch organization we did agree, however. While we welcomed the company and the assistance of our visiting brother (and we were reluctant to create friction with such an influential man) we both felt that he was overreaching his authority. Much against our judgment the proposal to turn the mission into a branch went through. There was another authoritative source to be heard from, however; leaders at the church headquarters in Independence did not approve. I mention this incident only to show that, while church businessmen abroad are welcome in local congregations, they should not attempt to take over direction of unorganized groups with which they are not thoroughly acquainted.

When Apostle McConley arrived in Auckland the branch organization was left to the discretion of the church appointees. Elder A. V. Robinson and his family returned to Australia, and the street meetings were abandoned. Our missionary labors were to present the gospel of Jesus Christ, not to argue.

One of the notable advances made during Apostle McConley's stay in Auckland was that the Maori tract I had helped bring into being was typed and taken to the Standard Publishing House in Sydney. There Walter Swain set the type and printed several thousand copies for use in New Zealand. This tract by Church Historian Heman C. Smith carried the authoritative voice of the Reorganization.

Jason, our third child, was born in Auckland on February 8, 1925. Soon after that we moved to Wellington where I was told to try to open up the church work. I secured a hall in which to hold services and bought a house on Constable Street.

Our second daughter, Ruth, was born here. The payments on the house were heavy, and at times more than our growing family could afford with my limited allowance from the church. When an opportunity to sell came, we did; then we rented a place on Island Bay, a fishing suburb. The Bay had a fishing boat anchorage for deep sealine fishermen who brought in tons of fish to be sold at the city market. For the purpose of good marketing, a streetcar service was maintained from the center of the city of Wellington to the beach.

About this time I began to suffer ill health. The pain centered in my left hip with the result that some days I was unable to get out of bed. When I felt well enough to do so I would go with the family to the beach. The sunshine and surf bathing seemed to help in restoring my limb to usefulness.

Still another health problem began to assail us. Our son, Jason, was a very large child at birth. For three

129

months we endured his constant crying without knowing that his mother was not producing sufficient milk for his needs. Finally, when we were both at our wits' end, we took him to a hospital in Auckland where personnel discovered that he was simply not getting enough to eat. The proper treatment at the hospital partly corrected the feeding problem, but as he grew older, his legs were not strong enough to carry him and his knees began to turn outward. He seemed healthy otherwise and grew normally as do other children. In fact, he was a very active child.

As we walked on the beach with him, we soon became aware that his crooked legs were a matter of curiosity to others. One Sunday afternoon we were strolling along Island Bay with the children when we were approached by a couple of complete strangers. They were very pointed in their criticism, informing us that it was a disgrace for parents to take a deformed child to a public beach. They had many suggestions for curing our toddler; they even told us of a specialist who could undoubtedly correct the boy's legs by operation.

My first impulse was anger. Then I began to wonder if these strangers were really interested in our son or if they had an ulterior motive. We returned home that evening filled with anguish and humiliated by the thoughtless criticism of strangers. We talked it over and decided to take him to the recommended specialist the next day.

On Monday morning we prepared the children for the trip to the clinic. Before leaving the house, however, I was deeply impressed that we should make it a last-minute matter of prayer. We knelt in prayer on the little boy's behalf as we had done countless times before, then I administered to him. As I did so the presence of the Spirit rested on me with this message: "Do not take the child to the specialist. Leave him as he is. Give him fresh fruit and vegetables, let him have milk and wholesome food and all the sunshine possible. If you do this, he will grow to possess legs so strong that few men in the land will be his equal."

We did not go to the specialist. The healing began to be effected as he grew. Later he practically lived in shorts during the summer months. By the time he was in grade school he was looked upon as a promising athlete.*

In 1927 my desire to learn firsthand how the Reorganization ministry was conducted in the United States resulted in my writing to headquarters at Independence to request a transfer from New Zealand to America. We had a little money from the sale of the Constable Street house, and we were a frugal family. My request was granted, and I was assigned to work in the Des Moines District in Iowa. Preparations for departure began immediately, and anticipation ran high. We thought of the United States as Zion.

Hilda wanted to visit her sister in Nimmitabel, New

---

*When he was graduated from high school, he enlisted in the U.S. Marines. He was wounded in Guam, returned home, and went to Iowa State Teachers College. While there he was rated by sports writers for three consecutive years as a "Little All-American" football player.

131

South Wales, before leaving that part of the world. She took the little girls and went by steamship to Melbourne; this sea voyage proved unpleasant because of the roughness while crossing the Tasman Sea. Meanwhile, I disposed of our household goods in Wellington and took the two boys, Paul and Jason, with me by train to my brother's home in Kerepehi. There I left the boys with Cyrus and Gertie while I went back to Australia to see my mother and father in Tuncurry. This accomplished, I joined my wife and daughters and returned with them to New Zealand, where we finalized preparations for the voyage to the United States.

In making the move I came with two objectives overshadowing all others. I had had enough debate with Mormon elders to give me a reason to go to the bottom of the history of the cause of the breakup into factions of the church at Nauvoo in 1844. The second objective was to give my children the opportunity to grow up in a democracy free from the jingoism of loyalty to the Crown.

In early April 1928, we boarded the Union Steamship, *Aorangi*, in Auckland and set out for Vancouver, British Columbia. We stopped for a couple of days in Honolulu where we were met by Brother Gilbert J. Waller and were entertained graciously in his home. This was our first visit to an American community and my first time to stand on American soil. It was almost symbolic that our first meeting would be a prayer service. There I took the opportunity to express my gratitude to God for our safe arrival in this outpost of American culture and to

132

rededicate our lives, as a family, to the principles of truth and liberty.

Later that night, while sleeping in the home of Brother Ralph Hall, I had a dream of the future. It concerned the Prince of Wales, whom I had met once in Australia.* In the dream I walked and talked with the Prince of Wales. "Remember my sons when our country is at war," I said to him. This was a strange mixing of the old of our lives with the new, and I interpreted the dream to mean that, although we would soon be American citizens, our sons would see war on a worldwide scale and be required to take up arms in defense of the Constitution of our newly chosen land.

From Honolulu we went on in the same steamship to Vancouver, where we traveled by train to Moosejaw, Saskatchewan; Minneapolis, Minnesota; Des Moines, Iowa; and then Lamoni, our new home. We were met at the depot by Stake President Wilbur Prall when our long journey ended on May 4, 1928. Other church people accompanied him including Gomer Wells, in whose home we stayed for a week to rest before renting a house of our own just south of the railroad station. We discovered truly fine neighbors in the Pralls, Sister Martha Young, Bishop George Blair, and others.

Our little nest egg with which we had left New Zealand had dwindled with steamship and railroad fare, and we had less than three thousand dollars

---

*I had also seen his father, his grandfather, and his great-grandfather in my childhood years.

when we arrived in Lamoni. We were determined to continue our frugal way of life, so we set out to buy a home in the location where I would be living and working.

Both the Presiding Bishopric and the Stake Bishop knew our financial details to the dollar, so in a few days after arrival, Hilda and I went to the stake bishop's office and turned over twenty-five hundred dollars. We kept less than five hundred to hold us over until our next monthly allowance from Independence would be forthcoming.

The bishop offered to give his assistance and accepted our money with the stipulation that it be used to purchase a house for our family. Members of the stake bishopric kept their promise to give us assistance in finding a suitable home. Under their guidance we looked at houses—good houses, mediocre houses, and dilapidated wrecks. It seemed that everyone in Lamoni had something to sell. The strange part of it was that every house shown us was practically the same price—the sum that we had deposited with the bishopric.

"Mother," I said to my wife, "something is wrong here."

"What are you thinking?" she asked.

"That these houses are not priced according to value but according to what it has been noised around that we are able to pay," I replied.

134

15

Thoroughly disillusioned with the help we were getting, I ran an ad in the *Lamoni Chronicle:* "Wanted to buy an acreage with good water. A three-bedroom house required." The response was overwhelming. We discovered that half the town of Lamoni was for sale.

We finally purchased a house on Mulberry Street at the west edge of town. The real estate agent we dealt with asked for one hundred dollars commission, which we paid, and the understanding was that the owner was to receive twenty-five hundred dollars. The house was old but well constructed and in good condition with three acres of land and a big barn. We were happy with our choice, especially since we could have immediate possession. With a small amount of furniture, we moved in and began to make a home.

In September 1928, our oldest daughter, Ethel, started to school. Our youngest girl, Blanche, was born in October. We now had two boys and three girls. I was away from home on my work for the church and the burden of managing and disciplining the children fell on Hilda's shoulders. That is, perhaps, the greatest sacrifice a missionary and his wife have to make for church appointment. I was always grateful that my wife was resourceful in meeting our family problems alone.

For health purposes as well as economy, we always owned and milked a cow. This was one of the reasons

135

for having an acreage. While I was in Independence for fall conference I became ill; the doctor pronounced the illness appendicitis, and I entered the Sanitarium for an operation. While I was recuperating, Hilda wrote me that she had asked a church brother to buy some hay to feed the cow through the coming winter and that two tons of "good" timothy hay was now stored in the barn.

I remember feeling a great satisfaction that we were thus fortified against the winter that would soon be upon us. Hilda also wrote that she had asked a retired farmer, a church brother, to milk the cow, and he was charging her ten cents a milking. This disturbed me because in the country where I had come from people did such favors without pay.

Finally I was released from the hospital and went back to my appointment in the Des Moines District. Winter in Iowa came with a vengeance; two feet of snow covered the entire state. I was working in Newton and staying in the home of Brother Harold Shippy when I became ill with pneumonia. District President Clyde McDonald came to see me, and I asked him to perform the rite of administration. He complied, and when the rite was over I was immediately healed.

Before I could complete my work in that end of the district and return to Lamoni, Hilda wrote me that our one cow had walked out into the snow in search of food and died in a three-foot drift against the fence. The timothy hay that our obliging brother had sold us and stored in our barn was rotten; our cow had literally starved to death. When I got home, I gave the

136

carcass to a farmer for the hide, and we bought another cow. It has ever been a source of wonder to me why men will be so deceitful and how far they will depart from the golden rule.

The church reunion of 1929 brought a spurt of enthusiasm to the Des Moines District. Officers decided to hold street meetings in Boone; since I had done lots of street preaching in New Zealand, perhaps they wanted to try me out. Little interest was aroused. Feeling that it was a lost cause I precipitated an incident that had the desired result. We were holding our meetings beside a big bank, and it occurred to me that I could speak in parable. After I was introduced, I began to tell the following story. Pointing to the bank building, I began, "If I were to tell you that this business institution was cannibalistic you might not believe me, but morally it is true. You will find in the records of that institution accounts of foreclosures; some of them may have taken place quite recently. The difference between the cannibalism of this institution and the old Maori cannibal system is that the Maori eat flesh and the bank eats money; of course, its operators do not kill the victims before consuming them." A young lawyer belonging to the church told me later that he walked away from that meeting sick to his stomach. "And you will be a lot sicker, my friend," I replied, "before we get through the next few years of poverty."

My story of parable about economic cannibalism ended the street meetings in the Des Moines District—as I had intended it to do. Two years later that bank closed its doors and the chaos of foreclosures and farmer strikes occurred in that area as well as all over the Midwest. Perhaps by that time the young lawyer was beginning to arrive at the nature of truth.

Affairs at home went along satisfactorily for members of my family. It was a refuge for me to return to them for a breathing spell, but I soon began to see that according to the standards of living in the average Iowa home, ours was being operated below standard.

I attended the Centennial General Conference of 1930 and was astonished by the extravagance of some of our members. I also discovered, to my disappointment, that much spare time was spent in card playing and telling questionable jokes. How different is this, I asked myself, than the world we are instructed to come out of?

I soon found a young church appointee who had some of the same serious concerns that I had. We "spoke the same language" spiritually, and I wanted him for my friend. He was Blair Jensen, later appointed stake president and finally called into the Council of Twelve. I have an old radio in my home that was given to us by Blair Jensen thirty-five years ago. It was the only radio the children ever had in the home, and they thoroughly appreciated it.

Soon after we moved to Lamoni my wife was elected leader of a women's group. She also served as a church school teacher of another group of women. Through intensive study she became an authority on the Doctrine and Covenants. As such she frequently corresponded with Samuel Burgess, church historian. The correspondence of which she was the most proud, however, was that established with Eleanor Roosevelt. While this did not solve any real problems for us, it did help to bolster our morale deflated by the conditions we faced daily.

Not the least of our distress was the result of contention between leading quorums over the theory of Supreme Directional Control.* Some of the leading men whose voices carried weight led the opposition against the president of the church, Dr. Frederick M. Smith.

Apparent as it soon became to me and my family that there was contention in the church in America, we tried always to maintain a nonpartisan attitude. Sometimes it was hard to listen respectfully to each viewpoint without taking sides. We were accosted on each hand with representatives of both viewpoints. There were many things to try our faith in leadership, but we tried valiantly to keep our spiritual eyes on the message of Jesus Christ, which had never failed us.

We came in contact with Elijah Banta when we bought our home on Mulberry and Main on the west side of Lamoni. Our house had been built by this old-timer in the church who had had quite a remarkable conversion to the Book of Mormon. A lesson as to the effectiveness of prayer can also be learned from this man's experience which we found in a copy of *Autumn Leaves*. In Banta's case, as in the experience we had had in Australia and New Zealand,

---

*Supreme Directional Control reduced to its simplest terms amounted to placing control of finances in the hands of the president rather than the bishopric.

139

missionaries in the church were far more concerned with preaching New Testament Christianity than in exploring and explaining the Book of Mormon history.

When Elijah Banta questioned his elders about the book, they replied that the best method of finding out the truth of it was to pray over it. The Book of Mormon contains this promise: "I would exhort you that you would ask God the eternal Father, in the name of Christ, if these things are not true. And if you shall ask with a sincere heart, with real intent, having faith in Christ, he will manifest the truth to you by the power of the Holy Ghost; and by the power of the Holy Ghost you may know the truth of all things."

Elijah Banta not only took this literally but challenged God. He sought out a secluded spot and knelt in the quiet of the forest. With the Book of Mormon closed, he prayed, "Now, my God, if this book be true, cause that when I finish my prayer and open my eyes that the book be opened." He said his prayer and opened his eyes, but the book lay closed beside him. He then changed his plea. He prayed that the book which he would leave open would be closed when he opened his eyes. Again he prayed, but the book lay beside him as he had left it—opened.

Disappointed and feeling foolish, he picked up the book and started toward home. As he walked the Holy Ghost influenced his thinking and this admonition came to him: "You did not receive an answer because you prayed amiss. Read the book carefully and the testimony of the truthfulness you seek shall come to you." Banta had both his answer and a lesson. We dare not try to tell God how to reveal his works.

16

In 1931 the darkening cloud of depression overshadowed the church even as it did the nation and the world. A chain can be no stronger than its weakest link and more than one link that bound the members of the church was weak. Individually and collectively the Saints had not kept the law of God. They had been admonished to "come out of the world in spiritual and temporal affairs" and to "owe no man," which meant they must clear themselves of debt and prepare for what they had been prophetically warned was coming. The church, dependent on members for tithes and offerings, had laid aside no surplus to tide it over the upheaval that hit the social structure.

As a family we felt this keenly when our monthly missionary allowance check from the church was termed "not valid" because the Jackson County Bank at Independence had closed. We had laid in our supply of groceries earlier and received the cash balance of our forthcoming check from the church, when our grocer appeared at our door in Lamoni to ask us, regretfully, to return the cash he had given us the day before.

We excused ourselves and went into another part of the house to hold a conference. A week earlier Hilda had received a small sum of money from Australia which was her share of her mother's inheritance.

"We will pay it back," Hilda told me staunchly, and I was never prouder of her in my life. "Never have we

141

had to resort to trickery or dishonesty to make a living."

I decided to go back to the Des Moines District where I had made friends and to contact the district president of the church there for help in finding work. Shaking his head he gave me two dozen neckties to sell . . . neckties, when men everywhere were trying to get bread! I had been catapulted from an emissary of God to a necktie salesman. What could I do with them? Hang myself? My fiery Australian temper came to my rescue. I chucked them under the first culvert I came to along the road and walked on to find a less belittling job.

In Boone, Iowa, I tried selling groceries house-to-house—something people could use. This was not especially promising either, so I decided to return home and do whatever was available in Lamoni and Decatur County.

I found work in day-by-day snatches. The pay was slight—fifty to seventy-five cents a day—building rock gardens or doing carpenter jobs. Most of the time I worked and walked home for lunch. Fortunately my wife had always insisted on keeping a cow, chickens, and pigs. These helped during the lean years by furnishing us with milk, butter, eggs, and meat. Where I had once teased her about not allowing anything that was not useful for food around the place, I now expressed fervent gratitude. We had no dogs or cats, but every year I bought a brood sow and raised a litter of pigs.

The children grew up helping to keep the "wolf" from the door. The boys had a two-wheeled cart that they diligently pulled to the creamery each morning to get buttermilk for the pigs (a cent a gallon). Each day the growing pigs would drink six gallons of it. They also thrived on corn which was only five cents a bushel. Thus fed, our pigs would dress out at two hundred pounds when they were six months old. Since we raised and processed our own vegetables and had our own dairy and henhouse, we had good food for our growing family.

Unmindful of the depression that was pressing in on less prepared families, our children went happily about their school activities, including athletics. At last I had time for reflection, and I thought about the injustice of a mother having to rear her children alone while the father is away working. I believe with all my heart that when men stand before the judgment bar of God they will be required to give an accounting of the time, patience, and love that they have put into the rearing of their families.

On weekends I voluntarily preached at Davis City, the Downey Schoolhouse, Pleasanton, Andover, Lone Rock, Bloomington, Chariton, and elsewhere in Lamoni Stake because I loved the gospel and talking about it had become second nature.

In the fall of 1931 I had an interesting experience. A bridge-building gang was working in the adjoining county of Ringold on a large wooden bridge. Dick Milton, a mule skinner, brought this fact to my attention, suggesting that I apply for a job. I hitchhiked to the site a few mornings later and found a gang of men working on the project with varying degrees of ambition. As usual on this kind of job, some

143

of the men were working while others were doing as little as possible.

I found the foreman and told him that I had come to work. He asked me what I could do, whereupon I explained that I had had experience from boyhood up with anything that could be built out of wood.

"Go over there," he replied, "and help those men with the fitting-down and decking."

I went to work, and it was like old times with the Australian hardwood girders. I talked little and answered questions vaguely, and the work went along smoothly until noon when the engineer arrived. After a few words with the foreman, he strolled over to me and fell into conversation.

"You seem to know what you're doing," he commented, by way of openers.

"Sir," I replied, "I was born with an ax in one hand and a saw in the other. If you like my work, I'd be glad to work for you the rest of the fall."

"Where do you live?" was his next question, and my honest answer to that cost me my job.

"Over in Lamoni, Decatur County," I said. And then the truth dawned on me. On these projects hungry men living in the counties had to be recognized first.

"I'm sorry," he said. "I cannot hire anyone from outside the county of Ringold."

With a lump in my throat I picked up my jacket and headed home. It was late afternoon when I reached the dirt road running east and west between Mt. Ayr and Lamoni. On the south side of the road I saw a thicket of wild plums; I crawled through the fence and waded through the hazel brush determined to have some of the ripe fruit. Then I lay down on the leaf-cushioned ground to think a way out of my disappointment. I fell asleep and slept longer than I could really afford if I was to get back home before dark. The shrill cry of a whippoorwill awakened me at last, and the sun was almost gone. I got to my feet, and as I headed for the road I heard a car coming. I stepped out into the road and hailed the driver.

He stopped, but said sarcastically, "I never pick up hitchhikers."

"I'm not a hitchhiker," I shouted. "I live in Lamoni." My reply was lost in a cloud of dust as he drove away leaving me in the middle of the road.

Hot with humiliation and anger over this rebuff, I stood still with the dust settling around and over me and heard the faint chug-chug of an old car laboring up the hill. "This time," I muttered to myself, "I'll board and ask questions later."

I had no need to take these drastic measures for as the car wheezed to a stop, a man with a friendly grin invited me to get in. The driver was ebony black with a fuzz of white kinky hair.

I climbed in, and as we proceeded slowly up the road I looked around me. The backseat was loaded with farm produce—apples, pears, sweet potatoes, turnips, pumpkins, and a sack of black walnuts. It was my turn to be grateful and curious.

"Where did you come from and where are you going?" I asked.

"One question at a time, young man," he chuckled. "They last longer that way. I came from the lumber

145

mills out in Washington State, and I'm bound for my home in Louisiana. This is my last trip north. I hope to stay home now until the good Lord calls me."

"You seem to have done well," I remarked, glancing into the backseat. "How did you come by this cargo on your run south?"

His chuckle deepened. "Some of it I got by trade and some by pike and carronade, that is."

"Well, well," I answered, loathe to let the trend of the conversation die. "Where did you learn your trade?"

He said, a little sadly I thought, "My old man taught me my trade on winter nights 'twixt Maddox Fork and Dunkirk lights. He kicked me home and flogged me blind with the gales a'howling and the forts a'firing."

"You sound like the original flying Dutchman," I said, delighted at his wordage and descriptions.

"No," he said, suddenly sobering. "My grandfather was taken from his village in Africa when he was a boy. His Achilles tendon was cut and he wore irons on his legs until he was sold on the auction block in Galveston."

I was silent, and he went on, "When I was a kid, I stowed away in a lime juicer tied up at the docks in Galveston. We arrived in Glasgow, and there I joined up with a ship called the *Cutty Sark* and sailed with the China Sea ships for years."

The *Cutty Sark!* The very ship my own father had gone to sea on. Certainly it was a small world to people who got around. "Here is my hometown, Lamoni," I told him. "This is my house." I pointed it out. "Please come in and meet my family."

"Thank you, no," he replied. "I must get to Bethany tonight. I need gasoline. And if I can't get it by trade," he grinned as he prepared to start his old engine, "I may have to use pike."

As I watched him chug away in his old car my heart filled with a prayer for his safe arrival home and a prayer of thanks for the chance meeting that I wouldn't have missed. Then I went into the house and was accosted by my two sons who had been watching my unusual arrival from the garden by the road.

"Who was that old black man who let you out of the car?"

"A Samaritan," I replied while their eyes grew wide in surprise. "A good Samaritan who picked me up along the road." Then, of course, I had to tell them the story of the slave traders and the slave ship that brought his grandfather to the United States.

My disappointment in not getting a job with the bridge gang was compensated the next day when Lee Kelly came to tell me that the job of sextant in the Rosehill Cemetery would be coming up in a short time. He explained that Bishop DeLapp, who headed the cemetery association, had arranged for me to have fifty dollars a month for the six summer months while grass mowing was necessary. For each grave opened I was to receive six dollars, and for graves that included vaults eight dollars. The average number of deaths and burials was about forty-five to fifty a year. I was happy to get the job, for the cemetery was only a couple of hundred yards west of my home.

Now with a job—even a menial one—I was relieved. I sat down to supper with my family that night with thanksgiving in my heart. We had pork and bean soup, homemade bread, and butter to eat and fresh buttermilk to drink. We ate and talked of the day's activities, had prayers with the children, and after they had gone to bed, we lingered just meditating on our good fortune. A full belly, a warm bed, and a family of loving, healthy young'uns—what more could a man want!

"Mother," I said, "Zion is not such a bad place to live after all. Blessed is the man who can sleep the sleep of the honest, uncondemned by family, conscience, and God." Good health and right thinking are so much cheaper than doctor bills; but we have to work at it. The good things of life do not come by accident.

My first gravedigging proved to be hard, unpleasant labor. The grave was to be occupied by the old farmer who had charged my wife ten cents each time he milked our cow while I was hospitalized. I had to sink the hole between two rough boxes on either side. The weather was rainy, the ground sopping wet. As I dug down, the embalming fluid from the two graves began to pour in where I was digging. It was necessary to keep bailing out the stinking fluid as I dug. I barely finished in time for the mortician to take over. The funeral was carried off in respectable style, and the relatives departed with satisfaction that their loved one had had a beautiful burial service. Few people ever realize the effort digging a six-foot hole can be.

From gravedigging I was bounced back in a very simple way to preaching. Blair Jensen, then stake president, came to me requesting that I go to Downey school district, south of Davis City, where I had had a special request to preach to the congregation. These people had been constantly harassed by the Christians. The bone of contention between the Saints there and the Church of Christ group was continuing revelation. Our people needed the reassuring defense that the stake president felt I could give them. I went, sometimes spending a whole week with the people of that district, taking care of my cemetery duties in between. Church families there included the Jim Snethens, the Boswells, the McDaniels, and a few members of the Isum Perdun family. This was a good old Missouri farming community and those people were the finest to be found anywhere.

17

Two old-time elders, Joseph Lane and Tom Bell, had been active in this group, affirming by daily example as well as explanation the principles of continued revelation from God. The contention between the two denominations dated back to the beginning of the Restoration movement. In spite of the controversy—and partly due to the example of Joseph Lane and Tom Bell—we succeeded not only in uniting the members but in baptizing new converts.

Soon it became apparent that local priesthood was needed to lead the group. I recommended Otis Snethen for ordination, but for reasons unknown to me the stake officials did not approve my recommendation. I persisted, feeling that I was acting under divine impulsion, until he was finally accepted for ordination to the office of priest. (Now, thirty years later, it gives me great satisfaction to observe that many of the little boys who went to the Downey Sunday School and grew up under the ministry of Otis Snethen hold church offices.)

In the fall of 1932 and 1933 in conjunction with my cemetery work, I took a job of helping the Snethen and Boswell families build a barn. We began by felling the oak, red elm, and cottonwood trees that grew on the hills of the Boswell farm. They were then snaked to the building site, milled, and put into a large stock barn. On this job I was paid a dollar a day plus my board; for this I felt quite fortunate. I lived with the Otis

Snethen family and had a warm room and three nourishing meals a day as I labored and helped with the church work in the community. At the end of the week I triumphantly took home six dollars for my family to buy groceries.

So grateful was I for the opportunity to earn a dollar a day that I often went to the job when my helpers felt the weather was too rough. One day in the cold of February I worked on the barn, scooping off the snow so I could nail on the shingles. I laid two thousand shingles alone that day; I had to work fast to keep warm.

The next year brought another cold winter. We had a three-foot snow, and the temperature dropped to three below zero. The cemetery had drifts four feet high when I was asked to take care of the burial of a newborn child. I dressed as warmly as possible, took the little casket on my shoulder, and struggled through the snowbanks to the "Potters Field" where the child was buried. I dug the grave, lowered the little casket into it, said a prayer of committal, and covered the grave with frozen earth. I was in the cemetery all alone during this last rite. The relatives had not thought it important enough to attend the burial, and they never did say as much as "thank you" to me for my services. My face got frostbitten that afternoon even though I kept it covered with a stocking cap.

The frostbite brought on severe neuralgia in my left cheek and right ear. For protection from the cold and accompanying pain in my face, I grew a beard. One day I was on my way downtown when I met two little girls. I knew them both well for they went to school with my children and were from two of the most prominent families in town. When I met them this day, I spoke to them, calling them by their first names.

One of the little girls piped up, "My mama says you should be kicked."

"Why does your mama want to kick me?" I inquired.

"'Cause you wear whiskers!" she said.

Sticking one foot forward and pulling up my pant leg slightly above my ankle, I invited, "Very well. You come here and kick me for your mother's pleasure." The children did not hesitate. Giggling delightedly, they rushed at me and kicked my bare ankle.

"Now," I said to them, "I have been kicked for wearing whiskers. You go home and tell your mother that you kicked me for her." That they did I have no doubt, for two days later when I met one of the mothers at church she refused to speak to me.

Sometimes when noted people died and floral tributes were piled high on the graves, professional people would come to the cemetery and remove the baskets of flowers for wedding decorations. I assume these takers reasoned, "Why not?" Flowers know nothing of whom they serve, and in times of tight money, these people apparently thought it was better stewardship to take flowers from a grave than to buy them from a florist, and the newlyweds remained blissfully ignorant of whose grave had been robbed.

When the boys were out of school during the summer vacation, they helped with the grass cutting at Rosehill Cemetery. It kept us all busy, for there was much hand cutting and mowing, but these were the

152

happiest days of my life—working with my two sons and living at home. If there had been any way that I could have changed my activity so that I could have made a living and yet remained at home with my family, I would have done so.

My oldest daughter, Ethel, was by this time enrolled in Graceland College at Lamoni. I was on campus one day when some public function was being started on the lawn and learned that someone had decided that a seventy should be included in the program, so I was asked to give a short talk. I was not prepared with a speech so I had to resort to an impromptu statement. It came to my mind to tell a story.

"In Australia we have various names for hoboes. There is the professional hobo, who might be designated as a 'sundowner' because he usually stops at a farmhouse or a cattle station about sundown. He might also be referred to as a 'bagman' because he carries a small sway of blankets and clothing rolled up in a bag. Another type is the 'outwest' hobo—a term which is more or less an honor or distinction. All of these terms connotate the same thing in the United States—a hobo.

"This hobo was on the road in Iowa for several days and faring rather badly. One day at noon when he passed a beautiful farm with a lovely dwelling, numerous livestock, and storage buildings, he sat down under a tree to gaze upon the scene. Absentmindedly he plucked a blade of grass and chewed on its soft stem. At that moment the housewife came to the roadside where the hobo sat chewing.

"'Oh,' she cried compassionately, 'you poor man!

You must indeed be hungry if you eat grass.'

"'Well, madame,' said the hobo, 'I *am* hungry. I have not eaten in four days.'

"'You come right around to the kitchen door,' the housewife invited. 'The grass is longer there.'"

I'm still wondering if that self-satisfied audience got the message.

It has long been a gripe of mine that though all men are created equal and many churches claim to follow the equality taught by Jesus Christ, there are privileged classes in the churches. We gradually learned that our lovely dream of a time when there would be no rich or poor was a fleeting ideal. The innate selfishness of man that the light of the gospel and years of theory have not dissolved has prevented the development of a workable Zion. Men are still rationalizing themselves in or out of situations that touch personal sacrifice or pocketbooks.

I went to General Conference that year and attended the Seventies Quorum sessions as usual. Two issues seemed to bog the meeting down. One was "concurrent jurisdiction" and the other was travel. "Traveling" meant that the seventies under appointment must be financially supported out of the Presiding Bishop's treasury. At this particular session, the question of a seventy using his personal savings was brought up. The president of the quorum said emphatically, "No!" Yet my wife and I had used up ours, including her inheritance. I had received no financial reimbursement from any source during these years, and I had done as much ministering as any seventy on the church payroll.

154

The simple fact of being a member of the Masonic Lodge brought upon the head of President Frederick M. Smith much opposition. Some suggested the advisability of removing him from the presidency of the church. This was another aspect of human nature that I felt people should reconcile within themselves—the disposition to judge ignorantly another human being, thus casting him into a given mold.

Another incident of poor judgment had come to my attention two years before when there was a discussion about selling the church property in Nevada, Iowa. The Iowa District Conference of 1939 wanted to pass a resolution authorizing the district president to sell it outright. The opposition was led by a priest who contended that there were sufficient people in the town, including his married sons, who wanted and needed a place to worship.

I went to Nevada to make an investigation and learned that the group had one elder, two priests, and a deacon available to conduct services there—as many priesthood as a good number of the branches had—so I determined to discover why the church had been closed and was being recommended for sale by district officers. The building, conveniently located near the center of town, was well built and fully equipped, though it had been sadly neglected. We decided to hold a meeting to ascertain why; I presided.

I began by saying, "You people believe in good publicity, I am sure. What kind of advertising have you been giving the Church of Jesus Christ when you allow this fine house of worship to deteriorate?" My approach seemed to put new heart into them. This was evidenced in the expressions on their faces and the unanimous vote to clean up the church, add a new roof, and again hold weekly services.

I put on a pair of overalls and helped with the renovation. While we worked I asked questions...and got answers. The services had slacked off because of the inability of one of the local priests to discipline his own child. The boy, about ten years old, insisted on playing around the building as we worked, making himself obnoxious; never was there a word of reproach from his father.

"There is the cause of this church closing in the first place," an old man working beside me whispered. "Those children were so unruly in church that everyone came to dread their misconduct. Many of our people just quit coming and went over to the Protestant churches in town where they could worship in peace." I knew then that the parents must be converted to discipline for their children if the congregation was to survive.

I invited the boy's father to come to church for a private talk. He came. When I explained gently what I had learned, he got very angry and indicated that he would handle his family as he pleased. Then I too got indignant because so much was at stake. Finally he grew more reasonable. After several talks to persuade the parents that they were responsible for their children's conduct, I was able to convince them that the child must recognize the church as a place of worship with certain requirements of decorum requested of all members.

When the building had been cleaned, painted, and

reroofed, it was a credit to those who worshiped there. Elder Claude Kress assisted me in holding a series of meetings, with the result that twelve individuals were converted and baptized.

In the spring of 1936 a number of released appointees were returned by General Conference action to full-time appointments. I was one of them, but the old fervor was gone.

The depression years, when we battled for a living while trying to support the church work at the same time, had left their mark of apprehension upon my family and me. While there had been no actual want in our home, we knew this was due to our own determination to overcome the handicaps of a no-money, everyone-broke world. We had had all we wanted to eat, but a degree of our health had been used up and our clothes and shoes had worn out in the process. Worst of all, our spiritual reservoir had begun to run dry. We needed a rebaptism of spiritual hope, energy, and love, and we had begun to doubt that we would find it.

18

A dream dies hard. We often remembered and quoted to each other the story of Jesus' ministry when the people to whom he was talking turned and went away because they could not endure his words. He said to his disciples, "Will ye also go away?"

Impulsive Peter said, "Where would we go, Lord? Thou only hath the words of life."

We agreed that here was a fact we must follow. In spite of our misgivings, we still truly believed that the church we represented had "the words of life."

The system in operation at that time was for the family to receive an allowance adequate to cover its needs. The appointee was, in theory, to receive personal support (food, clothing, and traveling expenses) from the congregations among whom he ministered. Under normal conditions this system might have worked, but I was in a position to see many situations where it did not.

It must be remembered that the people of the congregations were trying to recover from a depression too. Returning to my missionary assignments following the conference of 1936, I determined to walk cautiously in light of the five years of privation just behind us all. I needed clothing and shoes, but unless the local congregations where I ministered provided the wherewithal to buy them, I simply could not have them.

The new area to which I was assigned had more

than twenty congregations. Some of these were large city churches, but most of them were small town or country churches.

I have never presumed to be a professional preacher. My mission was teaching, whether from the pulpit or in fireside chats. Since I felt this was my specialty I had not given much attention to pulpit etiquette. It had always seemed a little superfluous to me when my first concern was to help men find God and to know the gospel in a way that would enrich their daily lives. Consequently, I had far more success in the country churches. I could help more people, and that was what I wanted to do. In their priesthood I found splendid men with whom to work, and the congregations were generally most generous in accordance with their means in supporting me.

In this district, however, I met another problem. My plan of ministry consisted of a two-week series of meetings with preaching every evening except Saturdays. I allowed this day for personal contact as I could arrange a time convenient for those with whom I would be visiting.

The church had a popular and well-equipped reunion grounds in the state, and the general officers thought this adequate for the present or at least until the debt of all reunion grounds had been paid off. In my opinion this was good thinking. The district president thought otherwise, however, and took matters into his own hands. He and his counselors wanted another reunion site.

As my two weeks series would be closing on a Sunday, the district officers sent out announcements of a weekend of district meeting. This arrangement automatically took the closing of my series out of my hands. Here would come the district officers to hold extra meetings not only on Saturday night but on Sunday as well—one at eleven o'clock and another in the afternoon.

These meetings often were not well organized or effective. Frequently they resulted in little more than an appeal for liberal contributions—presumably for the seventy who had held the series. The people were always generous, but the major portion of the offering went to the district officers. The district treasurer who was always present turned over what he thought I should have for my personal needs, while the rest went into the district reunion grounds fund which grew steadily fatter while I grew shabbier.

When I first became aware of what was happening I kept quiet, praying that this practice would run its course and cease to be. People in the congregations finally began to complain to me. They were resentful of the fact that the money they were offering to help me was going elsewhere.

When conditions got no better, I appealed to the apostle in charge. He agreed with me, said he disapproved of the practice, and promised to stop it. He may have talked to the district officers, he may even have warned them, but if he did they paid no attention to him.

This unfair practice was undermining my homelife, my pride, and my sense of justice. I was away from my family three to six months at a time. Often I did not have sufficient funds to pay my transportation home and back to my assignment. In addition, it had been my custom to give my wife board money for the time I was home. This was her allowance for personal use. Now with my depleted income I could no longer do this, and it led to misunderstanding in the family.

Little by little we all became thoroughly disillusioned. And to lose faith in an ideal is a traumatic experience. I came to learn that many of the seventies had similar problems or even worse, yet I did not want to quit. I had found God in the Reorganized Church, and I had found many fine, intelligent, and honest people. I felt I owed allegiance to them. Eventually I resolved on a move. I went to a member of the First Presidency, L. F. P. Curry, and laid my case before him. He listened like a Christian gentleman. In a kindly, sympathetic manner he asked me a few personal questions relative to my deepest interests. This gave me the opportunity to tell him about the vision I had had in 1911 when tramping through the Andes in Peru.

I explained that my life had been influenced greatly by divine guidance, and the sense of commission had not left me. I wanted to explore, understand, and develop the truth of the Book of Mormon. In a very short time after my visit with President Curry, I received a new assignment to the states of Nebraska and Kansas where I first met the American Indian.

But before leaving for my new assignment, the apostle in charge asked me to go to Rochester, New York, with Elder L. G. Holloway to assist in a debate with a Christian minister named John Page. I have never felt that debating was the correct method of

161

spreading the gospel, and I am glad that it is a thing of the past now. However, I will describe what happened.

The propositions for the debate were as follows:

(1) The Reorganized Church of Jesus Christ of Latter Day Saints is in harmony with the New Testament in origin, faith, doctrine, and practice. I, L. G. Holloway, being an accredited representative of the above mentioned church, will affirm.

(2) The Christian Church is in harmony with the New Testament in origin, faith, doctrine, and practice. I, John Page, being an accredited representative of the above mentioned church, will affirm.

Four nights shall be devoted to each of the above propositions with two hours for each night. The affirmative shall have two half-hours each night and the negative shall have the same time.

(3) The Book of Mormon is of divine origin and, thereby, worthy of respect and consideration of all seekers of truth. L. G. Holloway will affirm, John Page will deny. Two half-hour speeches shall be devoted to these propositions for two nights.

(4) The Bible is the final and complete revelation of God's will to man, and we therefore need no more revelations or manifestations of divine power. John Page will affirm; L. G. Holloway will deny. Two hours will be allotted each night with two half-hour speeches to be given by both representatives to this proposition.

Each representative was to choose his assistant or assistants, usually called moderators. I was Elder Holloway's choice. The Reverend Page had trouble from the first in obtaining a moderator but finally

162

succeeded in finding one from Cleveland, Ohio.

Attendance at each night's debate was fair. We advised our own members to be orderly, to avoid heckling, and to leave quietly at the end of each night's meetings. We were proud of the way our people conducted themselves by observing our advice from start to finish. Especially did we appreciate this attitude when we learned that the Christian minister's following spent time in debate among themselves after the meetings discussing what their representatives should have said or not said. This division was allegedly the reason why Reverend Page had trouble with his moderators.

The debate was to run twelve nights. After the first four nights of affirmation, Seventy Holloway began to take up the rebuttal, and I could see evidence of his experience and strategy. His consummation of the negative side in the eighth night of debate impressed me so strongly that I have never forgotten it.

He said, "Ladies and gentlemen, when the Bible refers to divine manifestation of the work of the Holy Spirit, either in revelation or personal divine manifestations of individuals, this man, my opponent, strikes at it. He does his best to discredit the personal testimony of living peoples as well as the divine record as written in the Bible." Then he quoted the words of Paul: "In the last days men will have a form of godliness but deny the power thereof."

At this point the Reverend Page, stung to the quick and very angry, jumped to his feet and demanded that his opponent apologize. Then he turned on me and demanded that I force Elder Holloway to apologize. If not, he threatened, he would end the debate then an there. Elder Holloway was a little hard of hearing, especially now in this murmuring, noisy room, so I wrote on a pad and handed a note to him. "Do not apologize," I wrote. "It is better that we end this debate now. It is accomplishing only hostility." Elder Holloway took my advice, and the debate ended there.

Another incident that I remember vividly occurred at a Kirtland Temple reunion. A Latin American doctor had requested baptism. He preferred to be baptized and confirmed by a member of the Melchisedec priesthood. This, of course, was not difficult as there were many of that order in attendance at the reunion. I was assigned to officiate.

A small group of people accompanied us to the beautiful running stream, the Chagrin River, just below the Temple. We gathered around a lovely, clear, rock-bottomed pool. I was beginning to walk into the water for the service when a large snake, a water moccasin, crawled out of the bottom of the pool on to a rock beside the water. Spectators at the service became fearful that the snake would attack. I advised them to be quiet, let the reptile alone, and regard it as a good omen that God had a work to do among the Latin Americans. Wherever the gospel was carried, I explained, we could expect to meet the forces of evil as symbolized by the serpent on the rock. The incident emphasized a truth. A serpent on the rock is unpredictable as to the way he will go. So are the ways of the world unpredictable. The gospel of Jesus Christ is the divine plan for salvation.

164

19

There is a certain finesse to the ordinance of baptism—a right and a wrong way of conducting it. Thought and consideration must be given both to the actual submersion of the candidate* and to his feelings. Some ministers are not aware of this, and unfortunate incidents result.

I have seen many sloppy performances that left bad impressions on the minds of the onlookers. At one time a young missionary I was working with had been chosen to baptize some youths. The creek where the ordinance was to take place had a nice gravelly bottom and an easy approach, but the stream was swift. I warned the young missionary to make sure of his footing at every step, and I held the hand of the candidate until he too had entered the water and was at the missionary's side. All went well until the

---

*I found that the proper stance in the water was for the officiating minister to stand beside the candidate with his left foot on a parallel line with the feet of the candidate and his right foot as far to the rear as comfortable. The candidate should be instructed to fold his hands across the stomach and grasp the minister's left hand firmly. The minister should then lift his right hand and speak the ceremonial prayer, calling the candidate by name, then place his right hand on the back of the neck of the candidate and submerse the entire body. The position of the minister's feet makes it possible for him to submerse the entire body and raise the weight of it in a dignified manner.

candidate was immersed. The missionary lost his footing, and both he and the candidate went floating off down the stream. Fortunately a boardwalk a few feet away stopped them.

I have baptized people in New Zealand in a shallow bay where we had to walk fifty yards from the shore before we could get into the water deep enough to baptize. I shall never forget one young man who panicked in the water. I repeated the words of the sacrament and submersed him, but he did not wait for me to raise him to his feet. He jerked away and struck off swimming under the water. He finally came up twenty yards away.

Most of our baptismal services were very beautiful and impressive. In the fall of 1945 I baptized four adult Omaha Indians in the Missouri River at Macy, Nebraska. It was a lovely October Sunday afternoon. We walked through the willow and cottonwood breaks along the river until we found a sandy bar running out into deep water. The leaves, yellowed by a light frost, drifted gently down, and the sun shone bright and warm.

We sang "My Country, 'Tis of Thee," prayer was offered, and I led the candidates into the water. The last to enter was a woman from Falls City, Nebraska, and as she was raised from the water, she sobbed aloud, "Oh, Brother Loving, for years I have wanted to be baptized. How thankful I am to be freed from a life of sin!"

Under the power of the Spirit, I felt strongly that the woman should be confirmed at the water's edge as stated in the Doctrine and Covenants; however,

166

fearing criticism, I did not do so until the evening service. Somehow the mood was different; we had lost the touch of nature's beauty and divine content.

When my two sons, Paul and Jason, prepared to join the service of the United States, we found that they had to be naturalized as citizens of the country. When my wife and I had received our naturalization papers in 1936, we were told that all foreign-born children automatically became citizens of the U.S.A. Now, in time of war, we learned that this was not true. We had to furnish copies of their birth certificates, which proved to be a difficult task. In 1928 when we crossed the border at North Portal, Canada, we had surrendered all birth certificates to the U.S. Immigration officials. We wrote to many government offices trying to ascertain where the originals were kept, but no one seemed to know. Finally my wife wrote to Mrs. Franklin D. Roosevelt in desperation. Mrs. Roosevelt responded promptly with instructions to write to the government office in Philadelphia, Pennsylvania.

Some branches of the military service were closed to the boys because they were foreign born. A top-brass military dignitary came to deliver a lecture one evening in the Lamoni Coliseum. During the meeting, thinking to get some information we could use, I asked him some questions concerning how to go about getting the boys' birth certificates. In reply he referred to me and my family as "enemy aliens." This brought a storm of protest, led by Art Lane of Lamoni, who stood up and corrected the speaker. We were naturalized citizens whose sons were trying to find a way to serve their new country, he told the man. Sometimes, we discovered, it is as hard to get in as it is to get out.

Jason enlisted as soon as possible in the Marines. He took his boot training in San Diego, was allowed a leave (which he spent at home), and returned to San Diego. He was shipped to Bougainville Island and fought through the tail end of that campaign. He was wounded while serving with the Third Marine Division on Guam.

Paul's military career was different. He was twenty and a graduate of Graceland College when his papers were cleared. A group of Lamoni people sent a petition to the Des Moines Military Command requesting that Paul be allowed to take the V.I. training program. The petition was honored, and Paul took the training which led to his being an ensign in the Navy.

Before the boys left for their stations, I had a father-son talk with them. I tried to explain that their service would not be as easy as a football game. All that I asked was that they stand firm and endure to the end. I wanted to get across to them that it would be better to die on a battlefield than to come home with a dishonorable discharge. They agreed wholeheartedly.

We encountered another bit of discrimination when I appealed to the chairman of the gas rationing board to obtain gasoline so we could drive to the wedding of our son, Paul, who was to be married while home on leave from the Navy. It was my contention that since he was serving in the U.S. Navy, the least the gas rationing board could do was to allow us enough gasoline to get to Kansas City and back. (It was common knowledge that the chairman of the rationing committee and his wife drove freely wherever they wished.) Words were useless; he simply would not extend us this courtesy, so we rode the bus to the wedding at which I officiated.

The matter might have ended there had not the offender got caught in his own act of selfishness. To get revenge on me for giving him the facts during the argument over the gasoline, he reported me to the stake president of my present ministry. When the call came to report to the official's office I told myself that I could smell gasoline . . . and I was right. The church businessman who had denied us the ration of gasoline was now pressuring me to apologize for asking for it the way I did. I explained that I did not think we needed to involve a third party since this matter was between the two of us, whereupon my accuser left the stake president's office in a huff without presenting his case.

A few days later the stake president again called me on the phone asking me to appear. I did and discovered that the incident was still hanging fire. I asked the stake president to withdraw from his own office and let the two of us settle this once and for all. He did. Within five minutes, after I had cited the law to him, the businessman and I shook hands and agreed to forget the whole misunderstanding and go back to working for Jesus Christ. Most of this kind of thing is done with the tongue, which according to the Bible is "an unruly member that kindleth a great fire." In church life, as in the Army, any man accused by the

169

top brass has a very difficult time getting to the bottom of an accusation either to admit he is guilty or to establish his innocence.

Shortly after the two boys had gone into the service, we sold our house in Lamoni and went to our new assignment among the Indians of Nebraska and Kansas establishing our home in Omaha. While working in my missionary field in southwest Kansas, I went to Independence, Missouri, to call on an old friend with whom I had worked in New Zealand.

Alma Barmore had been in the Australian mission in 1908 and had been married there. Now he was very ill in his home in Independence. After a half-hour's visit with him and his wife, I was preparing to go when he asked me to pray. His good wife and I knelt beside his bed while I offered a prayer for God's blessing and watchcare upon them as a family. Then Mrs. Barmore indicated that she wanted to pray. She prayed for me and my family, especially the boys in the theater of war. Her prayer was very comforting, for as she prayed for Jason I received the spiritual assurance that he would come out of the holocaust as sound of body as he was when he went away.

I was working in southwest Kansas when a dread telegram came. On an evening in August 1944 Hilda phoned me and read the cablegram; her sorrow was so great that she could hardly talk. Jason had been wounded in action, but the extent of his injury was not mentioned. Through the weight of concern there came again to me the witness of the Holy Spirit, and I was able to reassure her that our son would be coming home to us well and strong.

170

At the close of the war, Jason came home exactly as I had been divinely assured—well and sound. After a week's rest at home, he went to work in Omaha with a construction crew. The work was hard, but his mother fed him well, and he quickly recovered from the small amount of battle-weariness he had sustained. We learned later that my youngest brother, Amos Loving, was serving with the First Australian Workshop (Floating) Division on Guam about the same time Jason had been there, but they never met.

The following fall Jason registered at the Iowa Teachers College in Cedar Falls, Iowa. There for three years he was rated by sports writers as a "Little All-American" footballer. Thus he had come up through life from the small boy with the crooked legs to the young man who could endure the rigors of war and return to a normal, well-adjusted life through the guidance and mercies of God.

I have always been a nut for cleanliness and good grooming, yet I have felt that a man's clothes should be worn in accord with his labors. When I was on a job that required overalls, I was as much at home in them as in a suit and tie. If a church building needed painting or a churchyard needed cleaning, I simply put on suitable clothing and went to work alongside the people of the congregation. Sometimes this was especially needed as several of the sandhills of Nebraska where we had church buildings were overgrown with cottonwood trees. One might find a nest of squirrels, bees, or wasps making a habitat in some of the country churches. The important thing was for people to have a suitable place to worship.

171

But doing such work wasn't something I alone did. I remember a story from New Zealand. In the days of the Methodist pioneer preachers, ships from England landing in Whangrai in the North Island of New Zealand had to anchor offshore at a safe distance. The passengers then had to be ferried to the beach in lifeboats. The rocky shoreline made the first part of the landing possible only if passengers were carried on the backs of strong men who waded thigh-deep in the surf to reach the shore.

An English bishop was arriving on a ship that had just dropped anchor in the Bay of Islands. The resident pastor, the Reverend Martin, dressed in appropriate wading clothing, volunteered to serve as one of the ferrymen. He quickly recognized the bishop in his clerical attire and invited him to ride astride his shoulders to be ferried ashore. On the way in, the riding bishop asked the human ferry if he knew the Reverend Mr. Martin. Gasping for breath under his load, the pastor replied briefly, "Yes, I know him very well."

The bishop wondered out loud where the pastor could be on such an occasion, and the human ferry replied that the minister would no doubt be present at the public reception that evening. Accordingly that evening, dressed in clerical attire and presiding over the welcoming function planned for the bishop's honor, the Reverend Mr. Martin's identity became known. The surprised bishop thanked the minister for his services.

Another story of true humility is to be found in *The Spiritual Conquest of Mexico*. Ten Franciscan friars

172

and two laymen walked barefoot and in rags from Vera Cruz to the city of the Lake Tenochtitlan (Mexico City) to prove to the Indians that they were a different brand of men from the soldiers of Cortez who had exploited them earlier. These men ministered to the sick and dying, sharing poverty with the natives in such a humane manner that the people were amazed. They expressed their surprise with the expression, "Mo-to-lin-ear." And when the leader of the missionary group, Friar Torbio, learned the meaning of the Nahua word, he exclaimed, "From now on my name shall be Mo-to-lin-ear!" The word means "surprise and amazement."

During World War II, while our sons fought on distant battlefields for freedom, we at home battled over lesser things. Rationing of domestic commodities hit some of us hard in spots and, I am ashamed to say, we not only complained but in some cases blamed each other. Even such an insignificant thing as missing pant cuffs evoked criticism. I was in Lincoln, Nebraska, holding a series of meetings. While there I stayed at the home of Doctor Baller, who couldn't have treated me better. During this time Sister Esther Schrunk went with me to help me buy a much needed suit of clothes. The pants had to have some alteration, for I am a big man: I also asked that cuffs be put on the cuffless trouser legs. The merchant replied that he could not do this due to the shortage of material caused by the war. I simply had to accept the suit without pant-leg cuffs.

I was in the habit of wearing a belt and suspenders, so my stomach wouldn't stick out over my belt or my pant legs slouch under my heels. This combination, innocent as it seemed, brought unfavorable comment from some church leaders. An ultra-fastidious critic reported that I had entered the pulpit on Communion Sunday wearing trousers with no cuffs and with my pants hitched up, leaving my ankles exposed (I never could stand sock supporters).

Another couple of incidents led to the culmination of this accusation. I went to Dr. Hal Merchant for some much needed dental work, explaining to him that I could pay only so much but would take care of the balance when I could financially do so. At this he said, "Why don't you do what the others do? They send their bills to the bishop's office, and I receive payment from there." When I asked him who was doing this, he named two of the apostles. With some apprehension I mailed in my dental bill to the Presiding Bishop, but the payment came back promptly. I had learned something I had not been told all the years I had been serving the church.

Next it was necessary for me to have dental surgery on my lower jaw. Following the operation I went to my home in Omaha and took to my bed for several days. I could eat nothing but liquids and was thoroughly miserable. In the midst of this suffering, I received a telephone call from one of the apostles who lived in the district requesting that I meet him at the Union Depot the following morning at ten.

By the time I had crawled out of bed the following morning, bathed, and dressed to make the trip to the station I was very ill. I got there and found a seat in the passenger lounge to wait where I could sit in a reclining position. With eyes closed and sprawled down in the seat so that my head could rest on the cushioned back I was discovered by the visiting dignitary, accompanied by the appointee-pastor of the Omaha Branch. Immediately after formal greetings, he began a tirade about my personal appearance. He demanded to know what kind of socks I wore! I thought he was referring to the socks I had donned this morning when I had dressed hurriedly.

"You have been reported," he challenged loftily, "for appearing in public with your ankles showing."

It was so ridiculous that, had I not been ill, I would probably have laughed.

"What do you mean?" I demanded, stung to an upright sitting position.

"Your dress is not appropriate," he repeated, "for a minister of the gospel."

My feet came down hard on the floor as I stood up. "You strain at gnats and swallow camels. I have no time or strength for your petty complaints or those of your spies," I said and walked out of the station and went home.

About a week later I received a letter from him ordering me to appear with him before his superior officers in Independence, where I was to give a good reason for appearing in the pulpit with no sock supporters. I replied to his letter that I would be glad for him to name the time and place where I could appear with him before his superiors. Then he replied that he was calling the whole matter off.

175

20

To put the fact mildly, my introduction to the American Indian work in the RLDS church was not only a revelation and a challenge but heartbreaking as well. Have you ever tried to walk up an icy slope, laboriously gaining one step forward and then sliding back two? Of all of this, I was blissfully unaware at the time I was transferred to the Nebraska and Kansas territory.

In the rural churches of this area I began to find the usual problems of free-lance, undirected missionary work among the Omaha Indian people. Added to this I came in constant contact with the nonresults of "bettered" lives on the Indian reservation at Macy.

I had read in church history glowing accounts of conversions among these people. Missionaries who had preceded me in the field had baptized approximately seven hundred persons whose names were on our church records. The facts of these conversions came to light as I worked among the so-called converts themselves. Apparently the earlier missionaries had been carried away with an enthusiasm growing out of the promises made to these people in and through the Book of Mormon.

This was the wrong approach, because to the simple, uneducated Indian this promised something for nothing. The government of the United States had been doling out to these people for many years, and they mistook the far-in-the-future promises made to

176

them through the Book of Mormon to mean that all they had to do was be baptized and the church would take care of them.

To many of them "conversion" meant taking something tangible—something they could profit from here and now. When this failed to materialize, many of them turned away embittered and worse off spiritually than they had been before. These people simply were not ready for the Book of Mormon. They had to be converted to Christ and right living before they could begin to understand their own history. The earlier missionaries may have led them to believe in him but, like so many Christians today, they chose to follow "afar off."

About half of these seven hundred recorded members were living in Omaha, where presumably they could get employment in the war industry. Most of them lived in the slums of North Sixteenth Street where landlords collected rent for dilapidated, run-down rooms and apartments and where tenants made their rent money in many ways. It was my assignment to administer the sacrament of the Lord's Supper to as many of them as I could run down.

I was summoned one afternoon to a ramshackle rooming house to help settle a brawl. As I entered, I inquired of the landlord which room the trouble was in. He replied, "Just follow the stream of blood to the room it is coming from."

His harsh attitude was, nevertheless, little exaggerated, and what I found in that room shocked even me. I went immediately to a telephone and called an ambulance and the police.

Another evening I was asked to come to a home and settle a dispute between a young man and his wife. As I entered the basement apartment, the young man, lying on the floor bleeding profusely from a wound on his face, cried out, "Oh, Brother Loving, I want you to cast the devil out of me!"

The devil was rum—which many white people also could not handle. I sat him up, washed his face, anointed his head with consecrated oil, and prayed over him. Finally as he grew calm, his wife began to weep silently...and the "devil" departed from him.

The sad part of this story is that after remaining at peace with himself and his wife for two years, he was persuaded by a visiting missionary woman of another faith to go to college and prepare for being a minister in the church she represented. He did. He returned to Macy, his original home on the Omaha Indian reservation, where he was financed with funds to build a church. There he set about ridding himself of his inclination to dishonesty with both himself and his fellows. He finally turned the church into a residence for himself and his family. When I saw him again three years later, he had been shot by his wife. He was sick, drunk, and helpless. I said, "You are lucky your wife did not kill you when she pulled that gun on you."

"Brother Loving," he said thickly, "maybe the Lord has something for me to do yet."

"He has," I replied pointedly, "and you'd better do it quickly."

"What is it?" he asked.

The time had come for straight talk, so I gave it to

him. "You will have to repent and clean up your life. You are the best example I have seen of the parable spoken by Jesus when he said, 'A man once cleansed and returning to sin is like a sow wallowing in the mud or a dog returning to eat his own vomit.' God can help you only when you choose to help yourself. Repent... turn from your sins and live the way Jesus taught."

Sometimes our efforts in honest missionary endeavor were hampered by over-zealous representatives of other faiths. It seemed to be the vogue then for all churches to want to convert the Indian; some of the methods they used were unbelievable.

My wife and I were conducting a church school class each Sunday morning in a private home in Omaha where the families of several members gathered. One morning while our class was in session a missionary from another church came in without invitation and told the children to leave. "These people," she accused angrily, "are servants of the devil!"

Our work among the Omaha Indians and in Oklahoma was so tedious and time consuming that I was finally given permission to labor among them exclusively. When I got around to the Oklahoma tribe I went in company with an older missionary who had spent much time and effort in baptizing the unconverted Omahas. There I found the same results. His responsibility was to introduce me to the work there; he thought this could be done in a week. Actually we drove from home to home for three days, after which he left me to finish the survey alone.

Here again I encountered the results of the

179

haphazard method in which the quest of bringing people to Christ had been approached. There was no doubt of the goodwill and enthusiasm of church members toward the Indian work—but the sad fact was that most ministers simply did not know how to go about it. All too often the results vanished in reports of numbers of baptisms performed and sermons preached.

To meet our responsibilities on the Indian reservation at Macy, my wife and I had to commute weekly between our home in Omaha and that picturesque little village in the Nebraska hills overlooking the Missouri River. To save this constant traveling, we eventually rented an apartment in the home of Charley Crum.

In time I became aware that the historical roots of our Macy Indian missionary work went back to the period of upheaval in the Reorganization. In some measure that confusion had carried into the administrative decisions. The Bishopric could not afford to build the church that a noted architect, also a missionary, had designed and was determined to build on the reservation. Against the wishes of the Presiding Bishopric, the man began to solicit funds on his own initiative from anyone who would listen and give. Quarreling, sidetaking, and general confusion ensued, and the Indian was caught in the middle.

The beautiful church building was completed, and it was a joy to behold. It was a gem set in the wilderness, for it was to be the spiritual life of an operation which we called the "model farm." It was built of hollow tile with beautiful stained-glass

180

windows, an upper and lower auditorium, and a gabled roof with a stained walnut ceiling over heavily polished rafters. It was furnished throughout with the best of equipment.

Behind the church on its gently sloping hillside was a cemetery plot. Across the road a spacious and comfortable modern residence was built for the supervisor. Away from the building site up a low hill ran an orchard. The hill was topped at the crest by a grove of Russian olive trees. Here was peace; here was beauty; here was a perfect setting for ideal worship and learning. But from the first, plans began to go awry.

The dirt road that led past the church in its convenient location midway between the little town of Macy and the slightly larger town of Decatur was replaced with a blacktop highway surveyed and laid down at least a half mile over the hill from the church. This left the church and farm isolated and difficult to reach in rainy or winter weather. By the time I had been assigned to this district, the church was practically unused, the lovely grounds were neglected, and the residence in a state of slow decay. I was reminded of the biblical warning, "Beware how you hold too much good in your hands lest it turn to worms and destroy you."

This was literally the case here. The imaginative and aggressive architect who had made the physical structure of this dream possible had been moved by church officials. Later Elder Bern Case and his wife, Julia, lived on the farm and for years gave willing and faithful service to the Indians insofar as they could.

181

The real purpose of the model farm was defeated by the Indians themselves, however, because they were not prepared to give service—only to receive.

Rash promises which they could not understand had been made to them. They were to share in the profits of the farm which would be a "Zionic" unit. Native hopes and speculation ran to flood tide. To the Indian it was like a gold strike. Everyone wanted to get in. Missionaries were little wiser than the people themselves. Taking interpreters with them, they combed the countryside seeking names of those who wanted to be baptized. An old Indian who became my friend told me that he had accompanied the missionary to act as an interpreter. In one day they obtained the names of twenty-eight candidates for baptism.

Without instruction, without even understanding the language in some cases, these people were baptized and confirmed in the English language into a church they knew nothing about except that, through its missionaries, it had offered them reward. They knew nothing about obedience to the gospel or the atonement of Christ for man's sins. They understood nothing concerning their moral and social responsibilities to the community. Echoes reverberated throughout those Nebraska hill valleys, "Nothing but words!" For that is what it came to mean to the disappointed Indian. And this, I am sad to say, is the kind of missionary work that too often has characterized our efforts among other native peoples.

Years before our missionaries went into that part of the state, the Presbyterians had built a mission and a school on the upper end of the great alluvial flat corn lands above Blackbird Creek. Their missionaries worked among the Indians for the Omaha tribe. Henry Turner, learned chief, told me that he was one of a group of thirty young Indians lined up one Sunday morning at the Presbyterian mission for baptism. The minister passed along the line of candidates splashing water on each in "the name of the Father, the Son and the Holy Ghost, Amen." This sprinkling did not stick any better than our later immersions because the people themselves were not ready. Yet out of the many enticed into the church, there proved to be some faithful ones. Amos Lamson, beloved by all who knew him, was ordained an elder; Tom Walker, a young Indian who had been educated at Haskell, was ordained a priest.

The case of George Dick, who became a teacher in the church, was a different matter. He strayed from grace by becoming tribal organizer for the Peyote cult. This was a new organization introduced at about the same time the people became disgruntled with the RLDS church. They called it the "Native American Church." George told me quite without shame that he was instrumental in organizing ten Peyote lodges. The members met every Saturday night at sundown and went through the ritual of eating peyote until sunrise Sunday morning. The effect of the drug was that the participants were not good for anything for several days. This kept the members away from church, rendering our attempts at teaching or preaching futile. I began to realize that this was the work of a lifetime if one were to accomplish any amount of reform. To meet the situation and to make ourselves one with the people, my wife and I obtained lots in the village of Macy as near the center as we could get and settled down in a two-room dwelling. There we lived for two years—too stubborn to give up, yet chaffing at the ineffectiveness of our ministry.

Finally, in utter discouragement, I made a trip to Independence to talk it over with President Frederick M. Smith. In the course of our interview, after I had presented my chief problem—the Peyote-eaters—Dr. Smith said, "Have you ever eaten peyote with them?"

"Of course not!" was my indignant reply. "And I do not intend to."

Dr. Smith looked at me quizzically; he was an astute man. "Perhaps you should," he suggested quietly. "Only in this way can you really understand what they get out of it and how it affects them."

This was a surprising statement to me, but I accepted the challenge. After all, how could I know how the color visions I heard about affected the partakers unless I tried it? When I told my wife what the president of the church had suggested, she was skeptical. "How can anyone build a Christian order of life on a religion that depends on the effects of drugs?" she asked. I was inclined to agree with her, but now I had to prove to myself that it was not worthwhile before I could condemn it in others.

One Peyote meeting I attended was in the dead of winter, one in the spring, one in the fall, and one in the summer. I tried this number to see if the changing seasons had any effect upon the worshipers. Actually I could not see that it did. The meetings I attended were held in three homes and a tepee. The most interesting to me was the tepee.

About twenty-four people were comfortably seated on scented weeds laid carefully around the circle inside the tepee. About three feet away from the door toward the interior a rainbow made of earth, clay, and sand about six inches high was built. This was in the center of the tepee with the ends of it about four feet apart.

The sacred fire was laid in the middle of the apex of the rainbow. A fire chief whose job it was to attend the fire all night was appointed. The firewood was a special kind, possibly poplar, cut in lengths about a foot long and split in two-inch thick pieces. Once lighted the fire was never allowed to die.

The wood was placed on the fire in such a way that it formed an inverted "V" shape. As it burned down to red coals, the fire chief carefully parted the coals and spread them into a moon shape within the base of the rainbow. The blaze was always blue, and there was very little smoke.

The meeting began just as the upper rim of the sun disappeared beyond the horizon. The Omaha "road chief," dressed in gaudy colored scarfs wound around his head and waist and followed by the peyote chief and the drum chief, led the worshipers around the tepee several times on the outside. The group then entered the tepee on the right of the sacred fire. Once inside, the road chief, the peyote chief, and the drum chief took their places on the ground directly at the apex of the rainbow. The worshipers filed around the tepee, taking seats on the scented weeds.

When all were seated quietly, the road chief took a

piece of peyote and, kneeling in front of the sacred fire, dedicated it, and placed it on the apex of the rainbow. This represented the female power of creation when so blessed. Then he took another piece of peyote and, holding it up toward heaven, dedicated it, and superimposed it upon the first piece. This, the male power of creation, so dedicated became a part of the godhead. Four short songs were then sung to the accompaniment of drum chords.

In this setting the worshipers partook of the sacrament of peyote. The peyote chief arose with dignity, holding carefully a little sack of dried cactus. He passed it around the circle giving to each worshiper as many pieces as desired. I allowed myself six pieces, thinking this would surely kill or cure me. (The road chief had been known to eat as many as forty pieces.)

Passing the peyote occurred several times throughout the night. Each person had an empty can or jar at his side into which he could expectorate. When it was filled, he took it outside and emptied it.

The process of masticating and swallowing the dry, hard peyote is an art that few non-Indians can master. You try to chew it, moistening it in your mouth with saliva, but it will gag you. Eventually, after extended effort, it goes down. The first effects are felt in the stomach muscles. (If you vomit you merely shut your eyes and gulp it back down.) The chemical contents of the drug must get into your blood before you can see the visions. During this process you need the empty can in your hands to catch the saliva filling your mouth. If you can swallow all of this liquid your "drunk" will be more complete.

186

While the eating and digesting process was going on, the drum was passed from one to another. Each person sang or chanted four songs while his nearest associate drummed for him. At midnight a recess was called. Everyone arose and went out of the tepee to breathe the fresh, clean air. For this I was very grateful. As we stepped out of the tepee there was a fire burning in the shape of a new moon on the ground in front of us. This fire had been transferred from the sacred fire in the tepee.

After the recess the meeting was resumed with vigor. Peyote was passed frequently and eaten. As I sat there gazing into the blue blaze of the sacred fire, a sort of hypnosis came over me with colored visions arising out of the fire. As I became stupid under the effects of the drug, I became an Indian. Social distinctions and cultural differences vanished. I actually saw the ancestors of those Indians going back hundreds of years. I saw unclaimed forests, mountains, and jungles. There was nothing either uplifting or degrading in the visions I saw.

In the initial ceremony the two pieces of peyote were dedicated by prayer and became part of an alleged godhead to be used as a symbol of the sacrament. Under the drug influence the road chief at times sought out a woman and a man from the circle and said to them, "Father Peyote commands that this man shall take this woman...." Following these instructions the man and woman so designated arose and left the tepee.

Shortly before daylight a woman came into the tepee with a bucket of water. Sitting beside the door she began to pray in a plaintive, seductive voice. After the prayer she took the water and passed it around. Each worshiper drank from the same cup. The woman withdrew when this ritual was finished. Then a bowl of parched corn with syrup over it, sweet cookies, and a dish of fruit salad were passed in that order. Each person kept the dish before him until he had eaten what he wanted. After a few more rounds of drumming and chanting the meeting was dismissed by the road chief with a short prayer. We all stepped out into the first rays of the morning sun.

The fourth and last meeting I attended was in the month of July. This was held in a private home in Macy. Because of the heat I drank a lot of water. About two o'clock in the morning I learned from experience that peyote and water do not mix. I had eaten four pieces of the stuff when I became violently ill and had to leave. The physical reaction to my nervous system was intense. I lost control of the muscles of my arms and legs, my speech was slurred, and my tongue was useless for articulation. It took me several days to recover.

The distressing thing is that this drug is ignorantly given for illnesses. Peyote meetings have been assembled in families where there is illness and a medical doctor is needed. There the peyoters pray for the recovery of the sick. Often a tea is made from the herb and fed to small babies with a prayer that God will heal the afflicted one. Sometimes a peyote meeting is held when some loved Indian dies. This is a friendly gesture of esteem shown the dead and not in any way compulsory if the family objects.

I had many illuminating talks with Dr. Levey, head physician of the government hospital for the Omaha and Winnebago tribes located at Winnebago, Nebraska. He explained much about the effects of peyote from the medical viewpoint. At one time he had seen a man die as a result of its use. The chemical content is the drug mescaline which is said to be non-habit forming. Nevertheless its influence robs its victims of restraint.

At the time my wife and I were working among the Omaha Indians, we were often apprised of some human being who needed assistance. The bottom roads were ungraveled and became a sea of mud in the spring and fall of the year. When called upon to help, my wife walked barefoot down those muddy roads where she delivered a baby for some Indian woman in a shack of a house. It was a common thing for some of the women to bear a child at two-year intervals, each child fathered by a different man.

All these experiences resulted in the feeling of hopelessness that culminated in the belief that most of our efforts were time and money wasted. We had labored two years among these people with the result that we couldn't even measure our progress. Since there were local ministers living in Walthill, Decatur, and Macy to give continued ministry as best they could to the people who asked for it, we were not sorry when our assignment was changed.

Elder Claude Carter succeeded me in the Indian work. He and his wife, Ora, bought the old country church from the Presiding Bishopric and went to Macy to live. They moved the church building piece by piece to a hillside location in Macy and reconstructed it. The physical labor involved proved too much for the gallant pair. While pouring concrete for the floor of the church building, Claude had a heart attack and died. The building was almost completed; he had almost seen the earthly finish of his mission. An Indian elder moved into the house made vacant by Mrs. Carter after her husband's death and was placed in charge of the work there. The last report I had he was still there doing what he could for the few who remained faithful to the covenant they had made to the cause of Christ.

21

My release from church appointment in October 1948 at the conclusion of the General Conference was not an unexpected event. However, following it I wallowed for two years in the doldrums of indecision. Feeling nakedly alone, I went back to Omaha to the solace of those I loved and those who loved me. I needed to reconstruct my thinking. I had thought in terms of Restoration philosophy for forty years, but if I was to be true to the larger vision—the cause of Jesus Christ—I must learn to change my habits without rancor or revenge.

Slowly the light began to push back the bitterness, and I began to see that actually this forty years of ministry had added up to a kind of victory for me. I began to count the blessings now at my disposal. I had not been "silenced"—forbidden to preach; I still retained my priesthood license; and I would have a small monthly allowance from the church in recognition of past services.

Then the truth struck me like a bolt of lightning. I was free! Now I could think and act for myself without censure or criticism. God could be my guide. The release had given me freedom to go where I chose, to preach when and where I wished, to pursue the study I had laid aside to enter the ministry. The vision on the mountain of Peru so long ago returned to me, made more effective by the experiences that had come to me through the years.

Repeatedly I searched my life from infancy onward and found within myself the quiet breeze of divine interest that sent me back to my original love of anthropology, linguistics, and archaeology. In the lean years, while living in Lamoni, my family helped me save up fifty dollars to buy a set of records and textbooks in the Hebrew language. I spent my spare moments poring over the text and listening to the records. Then one day while rummaging through a secondhand bookstore in Omaha I had come across an old Hebrew Chaldee lexicon. I bought it for two dollars. Now I really began to learn things. *Schofield's Reference System* of the King James Bible and the old lexicon, plus the Hebrew linguaphone, opened a new world to me. I could study in a number of areas.

My dear wife Hilda, who had upheld me so many years in rearing and providing for our family while I was out on assignment for the church, began a gradual decline in health.

After we left the reservations of the Omaha and Oklahoma Indians, she returned to our home in Omaha and began adding to the family income. Our daughter, Ethel, at that time was in the University of Iowa at Iowa City and near graduation in the field of dental surgery. Hilda first went to work in a laundry to help with Ethel's college expenses, but the work proved to be too hard for her. Later she got a job in an overall factory as a seamstress. This, along with her abilities to make a little go a long way, tided us over until Ethel received her degree.

Ethel later married Dr. Rogelio Diaz Guerrero who came to Iowa City on a Benjamin Franklin scholarship from Mexico City. He stayed with the university long enough to earn both his master's and Ph.D. degrees in philosophy.

Blanche, our youngest daughter, had graduated from high school in Omaha with national honors which entitled her to study in the American Institute of Commerce in Davenport, Iowa. Later, with a basketball team representing that institution, she toured many Latin American countries. She finally decided to study at the University of Mexico, where she received her B.A. degree. Later she married Maurice Charpenel.

We visited the homes of our two boys, Paul and Jason, both of whom were teaching in northwest Iowa, until we got our bearings and sorted our values. The year 1950 found us buying a home on Savage Street in Independence, Missouri. There we obtained three large lots with an unfinished house on them. This gave me some outlet for activity while I sought work in Kansas City. I had been a missionary for forty years and had no specialized training in any other field. Only my native aptitude for building sustained me.

Settling into our home on Savage Street and being intent on making the best of every advantage that came my way, I located a job that fit into my home developing program. It also allowed me more time for Hilda, who was suffering from Parkinson's disease. The job was that of industrial police guard work for the firm of W. J. Burns, a detective agency in Kansas City. The work was not hard. As a night guard I had only to be on the alert for fires or prowlers; there was a minimum of checking to be made and reports to be written. I liked the job because it freed me to work at home several hours each morning. And it left time for me to finish the high school correspondence course that I had begun in Omaha. Without this schooling I would not be eligible to enter college.

I worked for this company long enough to establish Social Security payments. These with my church pension provided adequate support while I pursued my studies. Working steadily toward this end, I completed a rental dwelling on one of our extra lots in Independence, and my wife and I began doing a few things we long had wanted to do. We went to Mexico every winter where Ethel and her family (now consisting of two children, Rolando and Christina) lived and she practiced dentistry. I rented an apartment near their home so that Hilda could visit as often as she wished. We kept the apartment on Savage Street in readiness for our return to the States.

Before Hilda's physical condition reached the helpless stage we wanted to make a trip back to Australia. In November 1953 we began to make plans. While getting ready to go to the home of our daughter, Ruth Newhard, for Thanksgiving dinner Hilda met with an accident. While not affecting our plans, it proved to be a very painful affair. Going down the steps she fell and cracked her kneecap in three pieces.

We went to the clinic in Savannah, the town where Ruth and her husband had their home and law office. The kneecap was repaired and Hilda's leg was put in a cast. This was the way she endured not only Thanksgiving but also the beginning of the trip to our homeland.

We went by train from Kansas City to San Francisco where we boarded a Pan American plane for New Zealand. At Kansas City I checked our baggage, keeping back a small handbag for each of us containing the things we would need on the train. We were assured that our luggage would go straight through with us; however, when we reached San Francisco, it was not there. (The luggage did not arrive until several days after we were in Sydney.)

We boarded the plane and were airborne about eight o'clock in the evening. It was our first flight, and we were awed and thrilled with the new experience in spite of the fact that Hilda's leg had to be elevated continuously as we crossed the Pacific and I had to keep cold compresses on her knee.

Shortly after takeoff the hostess brought dinner. She paused at our seat with a bottle wrapped in a green paper napkin and placed a glass before us which she then filled with a clear sparkling liquid. We drank it with relish. After the dinner trays had been taken away, she turned to me and asked, "Dad, what was that stuff we had to drink?"

I had been waiting for this and was amused. "Why do you want to know now?"

"It sure made my knee feel good," she said.

Then I told her that she had had her first drink of champagne.

After a moment she said thoughtfully, "Well, that is the first liquor I ever tasted." And it was the last!

Our plane landed in Honolulu, Midway, and Fiji for refueling. We changed planes for Auckland, New Zealand, and landed at Whenua Pai (good land). Here we were met by a group of old friends and taken to the home of Alf and Molly LeBherz at Point Chevallier. Because we were still without luggage, I was fortunate to be able to borrow a suit of clothes and a shirt so I could go to church on Sunday.

After a few days in Auckland we took a flying boat for Sydney. Brother Clarence Butterworth met us and took us to his home. From there we traveled by train to Brisbane to see my mother who was being cared for in the home of my sister, Florence Peisker.

On the way up the coast we stopped off at Bowraville on the Nambucca River where my brother, Cyrus, and his wife, Gertie, lived. This was a very enjoyable visit, for it was the place of my birth and early childhood. We rode with my brother, Adolphus, and his wife down the coast to the Tuncurry reunion grounds. This place, too, was full of fond memories for it was the town where my father had been converted to the Christian life. It was here also that a dark cloud descended on the pleasure of our return to the homeland a half century later. A strange and elusive story of my release from the missionary arm of the church had been told—insanity.

At first my wife and I were shunned, sometimes completely ostracized, at Tiona Reunion to which we had so eagerly come. Having been warned by relatives of the gossip, we kept quiet and renewed old acquaintances. Until Thursday afternoon we had had no official recognition whatsoever. Then an old elder who had known me well for a long time asked the leader in the pulpit why a visitor who had been a missionary for forty years had not been introduced.

196

That evening both my wife and I were invited to the speaker's stand and introduced to the congregation, and I was asked to speak to the people for five minutes.

It wasn't much time, but it was enough. That five-minute speech settled for all time the question of my sanity. When the meeting closed, we were beseiged by well-wishers, and I received requests from pastors all up and down the coast to be a guest speaker at their services. On the spot I took out a little notebook and began to jot down each appointment. After preaching three times one Sunday in different cities, a woman who I had heard had repeated the gossip of my "insanity" came to me and put her arms around me. "Oh, Brother Loving," she said contritely, "I am so glad you are all right."

I could afford to be lenient. "I never felt righter in my life," I replied.

I will mention one injustice that came out of that reunion experience. At a prayer and testimony meeting we three Loving brothers—Cyrus, Adolphus, and I—sat together near the front of the big tent. As was our custom at such meetings, we all took part according to what we felt we were led to say. I was the first to testify, and I remember that it was to the effect that I had always felt it my duty as well as my privilege to mold the lives of my children by setting a right example in both moral and spiritual conduct.

When I sat down my brother, Adolphus, who was a high priest, arose to speak in tongues and give the interpretation. He gave an admonition for the young people to free themselves from the sins of the world, particularly the sins involving sex.

At the time no exception was taken to this advice. Congregations of Saints have come to expect some manifestation of the Spirit to follow the preparation they make day by day in humility and prayer. It was not long, however, until a garbled account of this incident reached the United States.

Without a hearing my brother, Adolphus, was put under official silence within thirty days; this remained in effect for eleven years.

After the reunion we returned to Bowraville on the Nambucca River and spent a few days more with Cyrus and his wife; then we went to Queensland and remained there until my mother died on February 3, 1954, at the age of eighty-three. We accompanied her body by train back to the Bowraville Cemetery.

Hilda and I visited childhood friends in Bowraville for several days. Here I fished for perch and cat in Buccrabendinni Creek. This freshwater mountain stream had been noted for its abundant supply of fish in my boyhood, and this was still true.

Reluctantly leaving this familiar and beloved part of the earth we went down the coast to Newcastle, a great coal shipping port. This was an old RLDS stronghold, and I had speaking engagements in three different churches. Here I finished my ministry before returning to the States.

198

22

It was a memorable and thoroughly happy day for me when I was accepted in the Mexican School of Anthropology and History as a student of linguistics and archaeology. Blessed with a tongue that could conquer foreign languages, I found that Spanish was no exception. I was determined to get a college degree.

In 1958 I studied and worked in Mexico City College as a student field archaeologist. Eleven of us went to the branch school at Oaxaca for the summer. I took my wife along, and we lived in the school where we had board and lodging as well as classes. Our fieldwork was located at Yagul and a nearby island called Caballito Blanco. College teams had been at Yagul a season earlier and mapped part of the area. We finished the mapping and went upon the tabletop of Caballito Blanco.

Some days we had classes in the school and attended various functions in and around Oaxaca. In the field each student was given a crew of five workmen who did the digging while the student supervised and recorded the findings. Nothing of specific importance was uncovered that summer; we did learn, however, that the site of Caballito Blanco was very old—pre-classic. Many shards were collected and taken back to the college for classification. I hauled them from Oaxaca to Mexico City in my car; the load was so heavy we would not make the trip in one day, and had to remain overnight at Pueblo.

When the summer course was over I put Hilda in the car, and we began the long trip home to the States. Her health was failing so fast now that I had a feeling she would not be returning to Mexico. I tried to explain this to my daughter and her family as we bid them good-bye. At the time Ethel did not seem to understand. Or perhaps, as is the way with hurtful things that we do not want to face, she was merely pushing the realization to the back of her mind. It was a matter of sorrow to me that the Diaz family appeared to be relieved at our departure.

Another and a different experience met us at the border. I had driven quite fast, hoping to get Hilda home as soon as possible. The American immigration officials, of course, had no way of knowing this.

So ill that the American doctor had refused to vaccinate her, my wife waited in the office for me to clear the way for crossing the border. At the port of entry I waited impatiently while the man in charge asked questions. I am not a patient man, I'm afraid, and less so under duress.

"Do you have identification?" he asked.

I answered in the affirmative and produced several pieces of identification. One word led to another, each of my snappy answers arousing a spark in him until he threatened to call the police. The heat and the delay increased by the harangue between us did nothing for the comfort of my sick wife. Up to this time it had not occurred to me that he wanted to see my passport.

I always carry a passport outside the continental United States but he had not asked for it for identification. It was my fault, too, that I had not

200

thought to present it. In his aroused anger, he refused to explain what identification he wanted. Finally, since we were accomplishing nothing, I went back into the office to stand helplessly beside Hilda who was drooping with heat and fatigue.

The official in charge of the office recognized the situation. "Mr. Loving," he asked, "are you an American citizen?"

"Yes, of course," I snapped. "That is what I have been trying to tell him."

"Can you prove it? Do you have a birth certificate, naturalization papers, or an American passport?" I let out a long breath of relief, went to the car, and returned with naturalization papers and passports for us both. The official quickly cleared the way for us, and as I was repacking the bags in the car, the chief of the immigration office came to us and apologized for the misunderstanding that had almost led to a brawl for which nothing but overwrought nerves had been to blame.

The rest of the way home Hilda lay on a bed I had made for her in the backseat of our trusty Plymouth. We traveled a few hours a day, then pulled into motels and rested more hours than we traveled. It took us six days to get home to Independence. By this time she was helpless.

I tried to hire help to relieve me in caring for her in our home, but she called for me constantly. Her illness had reached a point that she wrangled querulously all the time. Finally I took her to a nursing home. This had been going on for six weeks, and I was physically exhausted and needed help. She died on December 3,

1958. Bishop Walter Johnson, a lifelong friend and neighbor from Lower Bendoc, Victoria, Australia, preached her funeral sermon. Members of the family were much comforted by his kind words.

I made arrangements with a neighbor to manage my property in Independence, locked my apartment, and returned to Mexico City College to continue my studies. I had for years been pondering the possibilities of what might be found in the Valley of Mexico. Somehow I believed that it held the key to unlocking many of the secrets of ancient civilization.

I liked the college because, in addition to the historical aspects, it gave me some opportunity to explore both on my own and in company of classes and professors. While studying archaeology under Professora Espejo, I—and other members of the class—often went to the location of the pyramid temples for first-hand exploration of the foundations. My experience as an Australian woodsman gave me insight into the ancient method used.

Cortez and his conquistadores came into this area in 1519. When they crossed the Sierra Madre mountains rimming the great valley on the south, the city of Lake Tenochtitlan was a metropolis with two large market centers. One of these was where the Zocolo is now located; the other, farther north, was named Tlalteloclco. This major Aztec city had grown from a few shacks on the mud flats in the center of the lake. Begun in the thirteenth century, it had become a great ceremonial center with many pyramid temples. But where had these people come from? This is the question historians have been asking for centuries.

202

The Aztecs, with their shamans (wise men or prophets) had come from the north looking for an old homeland. They knew they had found the spot they sought when they saw an eagle perched on a cactus holding a serpent in one talon and devouring the flesh.* They made a treaty with the Chichamacas living at Atzapotzalco on the western shores of the lake which gave squatters rights to the Aztecs to go onto some mud flats in the middle of the lake and set up their hut homes. The annual rental of these squalid flats amounted to a few ducks and frogs taken from the waters. The amazing part of this historical account is the Aztec genius for reclaiming wet land. It eventually manifested itself in the creation of what is still called Xochimilco, the floating gardens, a true work of art and engineering skill. The mountains surrounding the lake were covered with pine timbers of all sizes which provided a bountiful supply of small saplings suitable for making riffraff timber mats; these were laid in the mud and sometimes in shallow water. The silt from the bottom of the lakes was then scooped up and thrown on the mats. Small narrow channels were left between the rows of riffraff mats and these, in time, became waterways for small boats and canoes. As the torrential rains of the summers continued to bring silt down from the mountains, the floating gardens grew in size and number. Food became more plentiful, and the people multiplied into thriving communities.

Avenues of trees with little foliage but deep roots

---

*This symbol is today the national emblem on the national flag and on the currency of Mexico.

were planted along the edge of the riffraff mats; these, in time, anchored the soil.* As the population increased, the city continued to expand. Markets and ceremonial centers became a necessity. To support the pyramids that were standing at the time of the arrival of the conquistadores, another engineering feat was devised. Workmen went to the mountains with their copper axes and cut pilings approximately ten to fifteen feet in length and up to a foot in diameter. These logs were taken to the desired location and driven into the mud to the surface level. They were placed very close, sometimes practically touching each other. On top of the thickly studded pilings, the builders laid a layer of shale rock about a meter thick. From this foundation, the pyramids rose to great height. When the great central pyramid was completed, human sacrifices were offered in a dedication service. Some authorities claim the numbers ran into hundreds of thousands. (Human sacrifice was the zenith of Aztec religious ceremonies.)

As the lake city of Tenochtitlan continued to grow, the Aztecs found it necessary to establish easy contact with the mainland and regions surrounding them. Once again they arose to the need by building two causeways of stone and earth. One ran from the south through the heart of the city to the northern shores at Tepeyac, where the shrine of the Virgin of Guadalupe now stands. The other was built from the eastern shore

---

*In the Aztec language these gardens are called *milpas*. Today in the region of Jojutla a term is used which is of pure Aztec origin—calmil, meaning "house-garden."

through the heart of the city to the western shore near Atzcapotzalco. Spaces in the causeways were allowed for the passage of water traffic, and bridges were built to accommodate pedestrians. The causeway running from the east to the west was found to impede the flood waters from the Sierra Madre slopes, and it was deliberately allowed to disintegrate. When the Spaniards arrived in 1519, it was almost in total ruin.

The problem confronting the university professors and interested students was to find a way to connect the later Aztec culture to the older culture represented at the complex of the pyramids of the sun and the moon. On the several field trips I made with the classes I learned that the uncovered areas were but a fraction of what was still to be excavated. In the time of its Golden Age, Teotihuacan was a metropolis with a paved area of more than twenty miles in diameter. The large population must have sustained itself in the fertile valley lying to the north of the great body of water in the lake.

Under the expert direction of Professor Pedro Armillas, I made a field trip with others in the class to the plains of Actopan and the ruins of Tula. I was most curious about this particular region for I had heard RLDS archaeologists say in lectures they had been told that in fragments of buildings left standing at Tula evidence of Free Masonry had been found. Since I am a thirty-second degree Mason of the Scottish Rite, I was anxious to see this evidence. I searched in vain; it was not there. This is another example of the grapevine method for learning which leads away from the truth, not toward it.

Professor Duran led another field trip to the hill of the star south of the city of the lake. I was put to work digging near the summit and uncovered a small ceremonial cement fire pit and altar.

I was so completely wrapped up in this course of study that my failing eyesight came as a blow. Reading became more difficult, and keeping up with assigned study became impossible. Had Hilda been alive, I could have managed. She had always encouraged me in my desire to learn and had she been in good health, she would have read for me. But I was alone—desperately and unhappily alone.

I sold my car and returned to the States for an eye examination. I was developing a cataract, the doctor said, but nothing could be done at the time. I returned to Mexico and continued my studies as best I could.

I purchased a Jeep station wagon thinking it would be appropriate to the rugged terrain I wanted to explore. I was only a half year away from that coveted degree, but I tried hard not to think of that. With what knowledge I had already acquired and my determination to see this thing through, I decided to go to the mountains and work alone. Fifty years earlier I had had a vision which had stayed with me—a vision that would not let me rest until I tried to uncover its meaning.

The nagging urge to follow geographical references found in the Book of Mormon would not let go. I wanted to locate the original Hill Cumorah where Mormon, the old soldier prophet, hid up the national library which he carried from the land southward in A.D. 380. According to the Book of Mormon, it had

206

been hidden in "a land of many waters, rivers, and fountains," a land that Mormon called the "Hill Cumorah in the land of Cumorah." This place has been designated by some members of both the Utah and Reorganized churches as being located in New York State. I do not believe that the complete library of Mormon was buried there. The desire of my life has been to find the truth, and to this end I worked.

Light seemed to be dawning in my mind that the state of Morelos held some key to the mystery, and the longer I worked, thought, and studied, the more convinced I became. With the possibility of complete blindness, yet carrying in my heart the burning desire to find the answers, I seemed to be led to Jojutla. There I became acquainted with some Indians from the Sierra Fria who told me stories of immense tombs and a large fortress on Deer Mountain at a place called Chimalacatlan. I decided to investigate these areas.

I rented a shack. There I sat down and took stock of myself and my resources. I faced the fact that very soon I would be hampered by failing sight. (I had consulted not only a doctor in Independence, Missouri, but one in Texas and another in Mexico City. All agreed that my trouble was cataracts; all were vague concerning the possibility of surgery for removal.) I tried a self-help treatment for my affliction along with much fasting and prayer. An old Australian aboriginal treatment caused the cataract to disappear, but the blindness persisted. It seemed at that dark moment I had come to the end of the way.

23

Many might say that I was feeling sorry for myself, and maybe I was. I missed my lifelong companion; I faced the possibility of blindness; and my faith in church leaders was shattered. I was low spiritually and physically. Only my belief in a just God was left to sustain me.

The Spirit often works in strange and unexpected ways God's wonders to perform, and it was working in me. Into this dismal picture came a young, pathetically unkempt girl. She walked in through my shack door and looked at me curiously. "What is the matter with you?" she asked in Spanish.

In spite of her impoverished appearance, she carried her head high. "You look as though the world had come to an end," she said.

"For me it has," I told her sadly. "I am alone; I am growing old; and I am becoming blind."

She gave her black tousled hair a negative shake and it fell around her shoulders. "You are as old only as you wish to be," she said wisely, "and it must be by choice that you are alone. You are a gringo."

It was common knowledge in this part of unbelievably poor Mexico that a gringo is greatly looked up to. To these Indians being a gringo meant having money—something that they respect very much as they have so little.

In the weeks following she came every day, and as we visited I began to realize how lovely she could be if she were cleaned up, and how much her native wisdom would be enhanced by education. Here is something, I told myself, you can do to relieve a small part of the misery and hopelessness you find around you.

"Juana," I said to her, "I am an old man, but I can take care of you. I can give you a home and an education, and you can be my eyes. Will you marry me?"

"Yes," she said simply, "but you will have to ask my brothers and my family."

She was following the rules of caution necessary in her world. Her brothers too were following it when they replied bluntly, "You will have to stay with her [they emphasized the word *stay*] and she will have to stay with you." The culture of Mexico is such that it is not uncommon for men and women to go from one spouse to another without benefit of marriage or of divorce.

"I am speaking of legal marriage," I reassured them. "I had only one wife for many years. Now she is dead. I will cherish Juana as I cherished her."

We were married in Cuernavaca by a friendly old judge. I was sixty-eight and she was twenty-two, but the matter of age seemed to bother others more than it did us. Juana Garcia Ortega Loving is a girl with a happy heart. Kindnesses to her bring out an overflowing love for mankind in a manner that is beautiful to see.

The July following our marriage I took her back to the States to prepare for and await the arrival of our baby. Our son was born August 24, 1960, in a Jeep on

Independence Avenue in Kansas City as we were trying to beat the stork to the Conley Maternity Home in Kansas City where prebirth arrangements had been made. We named him Albert Alborear (daylight) since that was the time of day he came into the world. We call him "Tito" (little Albert).

In infancy his life was despaired of because of a supposed heart condition. Thorough examination, however, proved that it was not a heart but a lung condition that was causing the problem. We appreciate the good care he received at the hospital, but I feel strongly that prayer prevailed where human knowledge ended and that his life was saved for a purpose. I feel that the prayers of his mother were especially effective, for she is a woman of great faith. I baptized her, and little Albert was blessed in church. He was fifteen months old and thriving when we returned to Mexico. On December 21 we arrived in Jojutla and found an apartment where we lived for four weeks. I then bought a lot and prepared to build our first home. Juana was happy—at last she would have a home of her own.

Juana is of direct Otoma descent, a vivacious and charming young woman who is proving what education and opportunity can do for the underprivileged. In our home in Jojutla she constantly ministered to the needs of those less fortunate. We had one of the few TV sets in the village, and each evening circles of children gathered in our living room for this free entertainment. Guests would come and go until our house seemed like Grand Central Station. Both Juana and Tito attended school and did very well.

I still made frequent trips into the hills looking, praying, and listening—many times on the back of a "seeing eye mule" (I had given up the driving). On occasion I would accompany tourists who sought an interested and at least partially informed guide, and many of these have spent the night in our walled-in courtyard in sleeping bags. The guest room was seldom unoccupied. Ministers, writers, explorers, and curiosity seekers have been among our guests. All have been treated alike according to their needs and what we have had to share.

While our hearts ached with a desire to help all who came to our door, our resources were limited, and we had to use discretion as well as pity in dealing with the poor. To be overzealous or unwise would be to reduce ourselves to the poverty level, for the need is so great.

The following example explains, all in all, the miserable existence of many natives, their desire for something better, and the inability of most to find it for themselves. I was strolling for exercise in the marketplace of a village one day when I was approached by an Indian who was selling wares on the streets. A small, ragged, shoeless boy followed the man as a shadow. Each was loaded about the shoulders with handmade baskets, some large, some small. As they met me the man began his sales pitch.

I was more interested in the frail-looking boy than in the merchandise. Although small and under-nourished, he had a beautiful face with soft brown eyes. He was watching me intently as though he was trying to read from my face my decision.

211

"Buy a basket, buy a basket," the man wheedled. "Buy a basket so we can eat tonight."

I had left my billfold at home. I turned my pockets wrongside out to convince him. "No pesos," I explained, "no pesoes for even a small one."

"What do you sell?" he asked skeptically, disbelief written on his face.

My combined Spanish and Aztec were severely taxed as I tried to explain about my source of income and the status of a retired man. "I am like an old burro turned out to graze," I said. "I have passed my time of usefulness to work."

"Will you die then?" he asked in sudden sympathy.

"Not right away. I have a wife at home and a little boy to look after," I replied.

He looked perplexed. "What did you do before you became too old to be useful?"

"I was a teacher of the science of God and human relationships."

He whipped off his old hat and stood humbly before me. "Can you help me to find the science of God?"

"Yes," I assured him. "I cannot find him for you though. You have to accept it." A puzzled look crossed his face, and I continued, "Before I can teach you the science of God I must know something about you and your life."

He bowed his head before me. I asked, "Is this your little son?"

"Yes, he is my son," he nodded.

"Is the boy's mother living?"

"Yes," he replied, "she is in a hogan in the wet country."

"Is this boy's mother the only wife you have ever had?"

"Oh, no," he answered readily and without embarrassment, "I have had three wives." He freed his hand to hold up three fingers. "And children—a boy by one wife, a girl by another. . . ."

"Why did you leave the other wives to take this boy's mother?" was my next question.

"My other wives were lazy. They wouldn't work. I had to beat them to get them up. I had to beat them to make them sweep the patio, to cook the tortillas and beans. This boy's mother helps. She helps me with the chores around the farm; she is a good cook and good businesswoman."

As the conversation went on I became more curious. "Are your marriage experiences according to common law or civil law?"

He looked at me sadly and shook his head. "How can people like us pay one hundred and fifty pesos every time we want to change a wife?"

At this point in the conversation a young businessman went down the street. "There," said my friend in triumph, "that man is married legally, yet he is a *coscoleo*."* A doctor, another businessman, and a couple of teachers walked past us. "There," he said, "go educated people. They also are *coscoleos*. They don't care who bears their children. It is the custom of the country."

And so it was. It was the custom of the country versus the will of God. This man had asked me to help

---

*A philanderer with women.

213

him understand the science of God, and I believe he was sincere, but without changing his thinking and his way of life, he could never discover the science of God.

Then a thought flashed into my mind. "Can you read?" I asked.

"No, señor," he said sadly, "there are no schools in the mountain where we live. The little boy does not understand Spanish."

I tried a few words of Nahua, trying to reassure them both that better days were coming. The words were meaningless. I bade them adios and went home with a heavy heart. I had been challenged, and the science of God had been challenged, and I had failed. I was beaten by a tenth century Indian culture in a twentieth century world of science. This man could not even read about a better way of life.

The frail-looking boy with the haunting eyes was growing up the same way. Education and jobs. . .if I had the power to work miracles, I would provide jobs for all men and establish schools for all children.

The manner in which we approach our missionary tasks among these people is mockery. We send out well-fed, well-dressed ministers and equip them with the best of transportation. Too much of their time is spent on pleasure like the tourists while the needy natives continue to pursue the only way of life they know—the custom of the country.

Still seething under my own inefficiency I reached home, gathered a few pesos, and went back to find the pair. At least I could buy a basket so that the father and little son could eat that night. But when I reached the corner, they were nowhere in sight. I had failed them, and they had sought their own kind. But what if I had helped them? What if the man had been repentant and cleansed? What then? He would have been socially isolated in a world of corruption—a condition that he most probably could not long endure.

I walked back home again, my thoughts still on the situation and the need. The solution lay not in the older generation but in the younger—in the establishment of schools and compulsory attendance for every child. The children must be taught a better way of life—taught to carry the message of love, equality, and opportunity to their own people. This was the miracle that must be wrought, and it would take several generations before the condition would right itself. The science of God put into operation in day-by-day living by the people themselves would be necessary.

I believe this will come eventually. It will come when every talent, every energy, and every prayer has been bent to this end. Meanwhile we can only struggle along, doing what little we can do to relieve the situation.

I have now accepted the fact that, as one man, I can do only so much, but I may be able to help lay the foundation on which others will build. Jesus said, "Let he who would come after me, take up his cross and follow me."

I have had two supreme visions: the vision of discovering the history of a darkskinned people in the mountains of Peru (I did what I could to follow that gleam) and the vision of Zion, the brotherhood of man. I will never live to see this a reality, but perhaps other men will. And who can say who will be among their number—maybe my own three sons.

In spite of all rationalization to the contrary, I shall face the day of judgment confident in the affirmation that the Eternal One has been my stay and my support throughout a long and varied life.